Next Stop, ETERNITY

Charles Kelly

LifeRich PUBLISHING

LifeRich Publishing is a registered trademark of The Reader's Digest Association, Inc.

LifeRich Publishing books may be ordered through booksellers or by contacting:

LifeRich Publishing
1663 Liberty Drive
Bloomington, IN 47403
www.liferichpublishing.com
1 (888) 238-8637

Because of the dynamic nature of the Internet, any web addresses or links contained in this book may have changed since publication and may no longer be valid. The views expressed in this work are solely those of the author and do not necessarily reflect the views of the publisher, and the publisher hereby disclaims any responsibility for them.

Any people depicted in stock imagery provided by Thinkstock are models, and such images are being used for illustrative purposes only. Certain stock imagery © Thinkstock.

ISBN: 978-1-4897-0740-6 (sc)
ISBN: 978-1-4897-0739-0 (hc)
ISBN: 978-1-4897-0741-3 (e)

Library of Congress Control Number: 2016904165

Print information available on the last page.

LifeRich Publishing rev. date: 05/09/2016

Contents

Acknowledgements

Thanks to James C. (Jim) Kelly, Bruce G. Kelly and Philip B. (Phil) Kelly, my younger siblings, who encouraged me to record what our father, the Reverend Charles M. "Red" Kelly, saw, heard and felt while he served as chaplain at the South Carolina state penitentiary.

A special debt of gratitude, however, is owed to Bruce, who did the tedious research to lend substance to these stories. Bruce spent over twelve hundred hours perusing archives and copying needed documents from the files at the South Caroliniana Library at the University of South Carolina and at the Library of the South Carolina Supreme Court. His search included microfilmed newspaper reports, trial transcripts, appeals records, letters to the governors and execution records on file at the South Carolina Department of Archives & History

Some of the documents obtained from those files have been edited to make them easier to read and understand, and excerpts from such documents are used throughout the chapters to illustrate the many phases of Dad's prison ministry.

The ladies at the South Caroliniana Library cheerfully offered their assistance and are due special thanks: Robin Copp, Beverly Bullock, Lorrey McClure and Ashley Bowden. Appreciation is also due the librarians at the South Carolina Supreme Court Library, Janet Meyer and Ellen Green.

The staff at the South Carolina Department of Archives & History is also due recognition for help in locating and supplying copies of official penitentiary records on inmates executed during my father's time as chaplain.

Special thanks, also, to the late Reverend David Wofford, who heard first-hand accounts of the executions directly from my father, his boyhood pastor. The Reverend Wofford never ceased to encourage the writing and documentation of these execution stories.

Some whose fathers were clergy colleagues of my dad encouraged me to write about those long-ago executions. They related what their fathers said about their visits to the doomed inmates during those inmates' final hours.

They are:

Earl Wells, a retired Knoxville, Tennessee school principal, the son of the late Reverend J. G. Wells, then District Superintendent for the Nazarene Churches in South Carolina. The Reverend Wells spent nights in the death house with my father and witnessed several executions.

Luke Gunter, a retired registrar at the University of South Carolina, and retired Lieutenant Colonel Harold Liner, who flew combat helicopters in Vietnam, provided information and materials that were most helpful to our effort. Their fathers, the Reverends E. N. Gunter and Harold Liner, Nazarene church pastors, also spent time in the death house.

Retired Army Chaplain Colonel William A. (Bill) Martin, as a young ministerial student, witnessed the execution of Willie Pooler, the subject of Chapter 27. Colonel Martin left the death house with a firm resolve to never again witness an execution. He described and reinforced my own horrific perception of the ritualized taking of a human life. He helped me to once again connect with the sense of agony that accompanies an execution.

The Reverend Darryl Bogatay, my former pastor and himself the author of *Daddy Can't Hurt Me Anymore*, a poignant account of his own childhood, was ceaseless in his quest to hear more of those long ago executions.

Kim Kelly Burton, my father's granddaughter, and her husband, Ken, are due recognition for securing interviews and obtaining news articles, pictures and other information on Clarence Bagwell in his hometown of Brevard, North Carolina. Bagwell is prominent in Chapter 2 and the subject of Chapter 3.

I am indebted to Jeraldine Paxton, who gave Kim Burton a yellowed edition of the now-defunct *Sunday News* tabloid. The edition, dated January 31, 1943, devoted almost three pages of coverage, with photos, to the execution of Clarence Bagwell and George and Sue Logue.

Bagwell relatives supplied information, family history, newspaper articles and old photographs. Those relatives are Joey and Ronnie Bagwell, Mrs. Betty Owens, and Mrs. Mildred Cison.

Michael Kelly, my grandson, solved and explained computer-related issues and often helped by doing word processing.

Dr. John Yelvington of Reinhardt University and retired business executive Pete Delin, my neighbors, read the manuscript and helped bring clarity to the narrative.

Introduction

These chapters are about the ministry of my late father, the Reverend Charles M. "Red" Kelly. My father served the Church of the Nazarene for nearly a half century in the varied roles of church pastor, district superintendent and evangelist and, throughout his seventeen years in retirement, he acted as interim cleric for churches without preachers.

During the fourteen years he pastored the First Church of the Nazarene in Columbia, South Carolina, he served, for a period of four years and eight months, as chaplain at the South Carolina state penitentiary. He received the appointment as chaplain from Governor Olin D. Johnston, and his prison ministry began on the first day of January 1943. Governor Strom Thurmond terminated his services at the end of August 1947.

Two years before he became chaplain for the multiple men's units in the state's prison system, my father witnessed the execution of two youthful brothers at the penitentiary in Columbia. Then, throughout the years he served as spiritual counselor to the inmates, he comforted the doomed and witnessed the executions of an additional twenty-nine men and three women. Twenty-nine of those executions were carried out in South Carolina's electric chair and three in the gas chamber in the neighboring state of North Carolina.

Background on My Father

MY FATHER, THE SECOND oldest of eight children, was left fatherless when he was only twelve years of age due to a hunting accident in 1920. My mother, Florence "Sue" Chewning Kelly, was the oldest of six siblings who lost their father to the flu pandemic of 1919, when she was just thirteen. Both of my parents had to enter the workforce while they were still quite young, and their teens were times of adversity. These experiences gave them empathy for other people who had struggled and suffered. My father's personal experiences made him an ideal choice to minister to the men and women serving time and those facing execution. He served them with genuine compassion, and he was committed to their spiritual welfare.

Sue Kelly

TO A CASUAL ACQUAINTANCE, my mother might have seemed quite tough, but those who knew her well knew her hard exterior hid a soft heart. Many times when my father returned home from an execution, she wept softly for hours. She was particularly upset over the executions of Sammie Osborne, Bruce Hamilton, and Wash Pringle. She felt that Osborne's punishment was too harsh, and she believed that Hamilton was innocent. She also believed Wash Pringle was innocent, and she wept for him, as well as for the four small children he left behind. She was a lifelong champion of the underdog and was elated when James Dunmore escaped execution. My mother was thrilled when Dad, who was spending the night in the death house with Joe Frank Logue, came home after midnight with the news that Logue's sentence had been commuted by Governor Johnston.

Dad Converted to Christianity

THE NON-RELIGIOUS, HARD DRINKING, cigar-smoking, nineteen-year-old Red Kelly, who grew up among the textile mill workers on the Granby and Olympia mill villages in Columbia, uncharacteristically attended a revival service at the Whaley Street Methodist Church that was located in the Granby community. He felt overwhelmed with guilt for his sins, and when the church pastor, the Reverend R. C. Griffith, opened the altar, Dad went forward to pray and accept Christ as his Savior, and from the time of his conversion in 1927, he never looked back.

He felt an immediate call to the ministry but did not have the educational qualifications for acceptance as a cleric in the Methodist denomination. Thus, following six years as a member of the Whaley Street church, he became a Nazarene, a Wesleyan denomination that allowed him to pastor a church while working as a grocery store manager to support his family. He enrolled in evening classes at Columbia Bible College to prepare himself for the ministry.

In May of 1934, he founded the First Church of the Nazarene in Columbia, one of the earliest of the denomination's churches in South Carolina. He would go on to become district superintendent for the entire state in 1947, and he stayed in that office four years. During those years, he was instrumental in founding thirteen additional churches throughout South Carolina. As superintendent, he originated the idea and led the successful campaign to raise funds, purchase acreage and establish the Nazarene Campgrounds near the small city of Batesburg.

Over the ensuing years, that camp facility grew to the superb facility that today bears the name of Dr. Moody Gunter, a prominent family name among Nazarenes in South Carolina and throughout the denomination. Dr. Nina Griggs Gunter, Moody's spouse, whom my father often playfully bounced on his knee when he visited her family's home when she was but a tiny girl, became the first woman ever elected as a general superintendent for the Church of the Nazarene, the denomination's highest office.

Dad was a masterful storyteller and, even when he was in his seventies, young people would ask the old preacher to come and entertain them with his delightful yarns and poems during their youth camps at the Moody Gunter Campgrounds. Dad delighted in telling his stories, which were humorous but always contained a moral, to those future leaders in the Church of the Nazarene. Among those forthcoming church principals were the sons of Drs. Nina and Moody Gunter. Moody, the son of the Reverend E. N. Gunter, who was the founder and long-time pastor of the church in Winnsboro, was at that time superintendent for the South Carolina District Church of the Nazarene.

Years after his stressful days in the death house, my father suffered from a disorder brought on by the horrors that he witnessed there. He experienced frightening nightmares that caused him to thrash wildly in his sleep and awaken in a cold sweat. He resigned as district superintendent during the Nazarene District Assembly in 1951 and became director of the Methodist-affiliated Oliver Gospel Tabernacle, a rescue mission in downtown Columbia. Following several years in that less stressful environment, he returned permanently to the full-time Nazarene ministry. He then pastored churches in Jacksonville, Florida; Fairfield, Alabama; and Raleigh, North Carolina. Following fourteen years leading the congregation in Raleigh, he retired. No matter where he ministered, his effort was a labor of love. He was a happy Christian who never spoke harshly or unkindly of anyone.

In retirement, my father returned to his boyhood home in Columbia, where he conducted Sunday services for church pastors who were on vacation and filled in wherever he was needed. He also served as interim pastor for the New Bethel Missionary Methodist Church, a Wesleyan affiliate in Shelby, North Carolina, for several years during the late 1970s and early '80s.

Throughout his ministry, Dad was an avid reader and collector of books on the subjects of history and religion. At the time of his death, his collection contained nearly four thousand books, and many of them were quite rare. To me, his love of books somehow illustrated his studious, genial and likable personality. Wherever he traveled, he made friends and, during one such trip, he became acquainted with the owner of a second-hand bookstore in Akron,

Ohio. The owner liked and trusted my father and periodically put old volumes in the mail to him with the note: "If you like these selections, please remit X dollars; if not, please return." Those tomes made my dad a well-informed man on religion, history and other subjects, and he drew heavily on those resources to garner materials for his sermons and youth camp appearances.

The trust people instinctively placed in my father became evident during a tour he organized to visit the Holy Land. During the first of two excursions, he met and became friendly with a local tour guide in Jerusalem. The Palestinian youth, after several days of directing the group, invited Dad to come to his home to share tea with his family. Members of his group tried to dissuade my father, but the young man assured him that no harm would befall him, and he wanted the Christian cleric to meet his relatives. My father went to the youth's unpretentious dwelling and was treated hospitably. My dad and the young man greeted each other warmly when Dad returned for a second visit to the lands of the Bible several years later.

My father was a devotee of the Apostle Paul and Methodist Church founder John Wesley. Abraham Lincoln, Robert E. Lee, Alexander the Great, and Napoleon were among his favorite subjects in history and he loved the humor of Will Rogers. His sermons on biblical characters were revealing, and some of those sermons received comment at his funeral. Army Chaplain Colonel Bill Martin stated, "You simply could not know the Old Testament character Job until you heard Red Kelly's sermon on Job." The Reverend Harold Liner, a fellow Nazarene pastor, stated, "The greatest sermon I was ever privileged to hear was Red's sermon on the Apostle Paul." From Adam and Eve to the apostles, biblical figures came alive during his sermons.

My father served many years on the board of directors for the Trevecca Nazarene University in Nashville, Tennessee. He served as a board member while he pastored churches in both North Carolina and South Carolina and while he was district superintendent of the South Carolina District. He delighted in conversing with the young men and women studying at Trevecca, and he followed the progress of many who entered the ministry following graduation, including Colonel Bill Martin in whom he took great pride. He encouraged churches to schedule concerts with the touring quartets from Trevecca, and he was pleased when he heard that some among the touring members went on to make their mark as church ministers and musicians.

Dad's Prison Ministry Gets an Early Start

MY FATHER ASSUMED HIS duties as prison chaplain on January 1, 1943, some weeks before he was to officially begin his service. Chaplain W. M. Smith unexpectedly resigned effective on the last day of December 1942, before Governor R. M. Jefferies left office. Governor Jefferies then asked my father to fill the vacancy.

Because of Chaplain Smith's imminent departure, my father had some involvement in the executions of John Robinson and Zonnie Frazier on December 11, 1942. Robinson was an atheist and a World War II soldier who steadfastly refused to pray, and he shares an interesting chapter with Zonnie Frazier, who died believing he would enter the pearly gates of heaven on that very morning. In addition, because of the Reverend Smith's resignation, my father also became directly and heavily engaged in the Logue and Bagwell executions in mid-January of 1943.

Prison-Related Duties

FROM THE DAY HE assumed his role at the prison, my father tended the spiritual needs of felons who were serving hard time at several of the state's penal units. His prison ministry also involved the distressing needs of doomed men and women as they awaited their rendezvous with death. His heart was broken when the spouse and four small children of Wash Pringle visited him in the execution chamber on the day before Pringle's execution. Destitute relatives of inmates were sometimes fed and sheltered overnight in our home. However, that was a risky practice and, following a situation with the wife and young son of an inmate who were spending Christmas in our home, there was no choice but to stop having such unknown strangers eat and stay overnight.

Dad's duties included visits to a prison farm near the rural town of Boykin. There, on a large tract of state-owned farmland, trustees with the necessary skills and knowledge grew vegetables and most of the meat and poultry that went to the prison kitchens. The guards' dining table at the men's penitentiary featured an unforgettable breakfast of homemade sausage, scrambled eggs, grits, and biscuits. The inmates ate the same food as the guards and prison officials, but they complained that the menu was monotonous.

News reporters who came to witness the executions sometimes received an invitation to come in from the pre-dawn chill and have breakfast in the guards' dining room while they waited to enter the death house. Following those hearty meals, reporters often mentioned the prison breakfasts in their accounts of executions.

My father assisted chaplains at the reform school and at the women's penitentiary. However, due to the demands at the men's prison, where he shared duties with the Reverend E. A. "Lester" Davis, the so-called Negro chaplain, he spent the majority of his time there. The main penitentiary housed adult males and occasionally women who were transferred to the death house within twenty days of their execution. The women executed during the years Dad was chaplain were Sue Logue and Rose Marie Stinette, in addition to Bessie Williams in North Carolina.

The men's penitentiary was inside the Columbia city limits and was located within several miles of the state capitol building, which housed the governor's office. That location made it possible for my father to rush from the prison to see the governor and express his concerns over an imminent execution. The chaplain used the open-door privilege granted him by Governor Olin

Johnston sparingly. However, he did use it several times to plead for the lives of black youths he felt to be innocent or when he thought the penalty was too severe for the crime.

The Reverend J. Harold Smith Holds Prison Revival

ONE OF THE MORE unusual events at the prison occurred when my father persuaded one of the most prominent radio evangelists of that pre-television era to hold four days of revival services in a small chapel inside the prison. Smith, a Baptist minister, had a huge radio audience for his broadcasts out of Knoxville, Tennessee, and his sermons were powerful. He was busy, and the chance for him to lead any such revival was remote. However, after securing permission from the prison superintendent to hold the revival services, an event that even the most veteran of the guards had never experienced, my father called Smith, who seemed fascinated with conducting a prison revival.

The superintendent would allow only morning services at the chapel due to the evening lockdown of the cellblocks, so Dad asked Smith to preach at a series of evening services at the Church of the Nazarene in the Granby Olympia mill community. Smith accepted and each evening, from Monday through Thursday, the Columbia Church of the Nazarene was packed and overflowing with people. Unexpectedly, church membership grew as a result of these services.

Dad Shared His Unique Experiences

MY FATHER FREQUENTLY DISCUSSED his prison experiences with friends and associates. In addition, his sermons at camp meetings and his speeches before civic organizations, Nazarene and sometimes Baptist or Methodist gatherings often included descriptive accounts of executions. His stories were in demand, and his descriptions were explicit.

The subject of one of these stories was Sue Logue, the first woman ever to die in South Carolina's electric chair. My father was also present for the execution of George Stinney Jr., a fourteen-year-old black youth who died in June of 1944 for allegedly murdering two little white girls. And the Stinney case continues to make headlines more than seven decades after his death.

As the eldest of four boys, I sometimes accompanied my dad when he visited various penal units. In addition, there were times when I went with him to visit prisoners on death row. I was also with him on several occasions when he visited a doomed inmate during their final hours in the death house. One such experience was a Thursday night in November of 1943 when Dad made a final call on Sammie Osborne, who died the next morning.

The Reverend E. A. "Lester" Davis

DAD'S FRIEND AND COLLEAGUE, the Reverend E. A. Davis, was a diminutive black minister, but he was a giant in personality, and he sang in a booming baritone. He and Dad became fast friends, and they often hunted quail together. Davis sometimes brought his superb church choir to sing for the Nazarene congregation in the textile mill community. Those Sunday evening concerts drew overflow crowds from throughout the city of Columbia. As fellow pastors and chaplains, these two clerics, though not of the same race or church denomination, were great friends.

The Four Governors

SHORTLY AFTER HIS ELECTION in November, Governor-elect Olin Johnston announced that my father was his choice to fill the position of chaplain at the prison. The gregarious and jovial Benjamin Davis, known widely as Uncle Ben, was a prominent grocer in the Olympia mill community and a strong supporter of Governor Johnston. Uncle Ben, who knew my father from the time of his birth, recommended him for the position of chaplain. Johnston, following a brief interview, announced that the Nazarene pastor would become the new lead chaplain for the various prisons.

My father served four governors during his years of ministry to the inmates, first Governor R.M. Jefferies, under whom he served for only a few weeks. He then served two years each under governors Olin D. Johnston and Ransome J. Williams, as well as the first seven months of his term under Governor J. Strom Thurmond. Dad never met Governor Jefferies but thought him to be fair and dedicated to justice. He was very fond of Johnston, a compassionate man who would personally visit the death house and talk with a doomed inmate or send a high-ranking state official in his place. Williams was dedicated to making certain that the inmate was indeed guilty, and, in several instances, he intervened with last hour commutations or stays of execution. Thurmond, a former judge, was more prone to believe that all defendants received a fair trial and should be sentenced according to the laws of the state. He would, however, sometimes grant a very brief stay of execution to study a case.

Governor Johnston Concerned over Method of Execution

NEAR THE END OF 1944, Governor Johnston dispatched Dad to witness three executions in the gas chamber at the North Carolina state prison in Raleigh. The governor asked my father to report back to him as to whether he felt electrocution or death in the gas chamber was the more humane way to impose the death penalty. Johnston wanted to inflict as little pain as possible, and he contemplated changing the method of execution in South Carolina.

The purpose of this book is to bring into focus capital punishment as it was practiced throughout the decades of the 1930s and '40s. I believe these cases illustrate that injustice was not rare and discrimination often played a part. I have not included the names of innocent people, such as rape and assault victims, in the case histories. There is no intent to embarrass anyone, and the objective of these chapters is only to validate, define, and bring awareness to the cultural conditions of that vanished era. My father, from his vantage point as chaplain at the institutions of incarceration, saw first-hand the pain that so many perpetrators and their victims suffered.

No doubt the reader will note that a strange love–hate relationship existed between death row inmates and prison guards. Several inmates, as they sat strapped in the chair awaiting execution, expressed appreciation to members of the guard staff who stood the watches in the death house. None of the prisoners, in my father's experience, ever accused guards of mistreating them.

Adoption of Phil

CHILDREN LOVED MY FATHER, and he loved the youngsters. To illustrate Dad's and Mom's loving and compassionate natures, I have included the unusual story of Phil, the fourth Kelly sibling my parents adopted just two months after my father left the prison system as chaplain and at about the same time Dad was elected Nazarene district superintendent, in the fall of 1947. Phil's is an inspiring story, and he is now a successful businessman.

The ordeals of my parents' early years left them neither hard nor bitter, as Phil's story shows. If anything, the hardships and tiring workloads they endured as children instilled a deep sense of understanding for all who struggled to overcome life's sometimes-brutal challenges.

Phil is the natural son of an unknown Chinese nationalist fighter pilot, an unknown warrior stationed at Shaw Air Force Base near the city of Sumter shortly after the end of World War II. The young Chinese aviator and a number of his fellow Nationalist pilots were in training to fly the most sophisticated United

States fighter planes of that era. The advanced aircraft, including some early jet fighters, were supplied to the Chinese nationalist military forces, which were in a desperate struggle against Mao's Communist armies as they swept across and conquered the mainland of China.

The pilot became involved with a local girl of unknown background, and Phil became the child of that union. The single mother could not care for the infant, and the unmarried Chinese father was in no position to take the baby back to his war-ravaged homeland. My parents learned about the abandoned infant, and their hearts went out to him. Just two weeks shy of his first birthday, in November 1947, Phil became the newest member of the Kelly household. He would bring unconditional joy and happiness to his new family.

Southern white families simply did not adopt Chinese babies during the 1940s, and Phil's adoption would ultimately spell trouble for his adoptive parents. There was never a problem when Dad pastored churches in Florida, North Carolina, and South Carolina as Phil was growing up. In addition, the Nazarene church members in Columbia, Jacksonville, and Raleigh treated Phil as they would have treated one of their own. However, my father became the pastor of a church in Birmingham, Alabama, and even though the church people welcomed the boy, who was then nine or ten, the Ku Klux Klan did not. At a Sunday night service, just minutes before the start of worship, a group of hooded Klansmen walked into the church and occupied the first several rows of pews in the sanctuary.

My father stood and walked forward to the pulpit. He took the microphone in his hand and calmly welcomed the Klansmen to the service. He said that, since they allegedly belonged to a God-fearing organization, he was inviting the leader of the group to come to the pulpit and open the service with a word of prayer. For a long moment, no one moved, and no one made a sound. Suddenly, one of the Klansmen, apparently their leader, stood and faced the congregation. He motioned for the hooded men to stand and, without saying a word, he motioned for the group to follow him out of the church. There were no further problems with the KKK. However, for the safety and well-being of Phil, who was then the only one of the boys living at home, my parents sought another church to pastor, and they accepted the call to the First Church of the Nazarene in Raleigh, North Carolina.

Prologue

The death house experiences my father, the Reverend Charles M. Kelly, lived through when he served as chaplain of the South Carolina state penitentiary were always ugly but sometimes miraculous. The chapters in this volume focus on inmates who were either executed or narrowly escaped death in the electric chair during the time that my dad served as spiritual counselor to the inmates. Chapter1 and Chapters 30-31- 32 are narrations of well publicized crimes and executions in which he was either minimally involved or not involved at all.

The executions in Chapter 1 occurred two years before my father becoming chaplain, and his role in the execution of the Evans brothers was strictly as a witness. My father also played no role in Chapter 30, which involves the murder of Captain J. Olin Sanders and the six executions that resulted. However, that murder was the headline-creating case of the 1930s, as was the Logue case in the 1940s, and the Bigham case of the 1920s.

My father became heavily involved in the Logue executions and was directly involved in the parole of Ed Bigham, the subject of Chapter 32. Bigham served nearly forty years in prison for the slayings of five family members, charges he always denied. Chapter 31 concerns the case of atheist soldier John Robinson and the separate case of a repentant Zonnie Frazier who were executed two weeks before Dad became chaplain. Dad played only a minor role in the Robinson-Frazier executions, but all three additional chapters add context and perspective to executions in South Carolina during the 1920s, 1930s and 1940s.

My father spent only five years of his fifty-odd years as a minister in the prison. However, those years as spiritual mentor to the inmates, particularly those who were executed, would forever lend significant and poignant definition to his long career as a member of the Nazarene clergy.

Heartache, Pain, Suffering, and Racism

THIS NARRATIVE IS ABOUT heartache, pain, and suffering. The chapters are factual accounts of human depravity, physical cruelty, mental torture, rape, and murder. To deny that societal racism was a factor in many of the cases would be less than candid. These stories, however, illustrate both the unjust racial conditions that were so prevalent during the 1940s and the extreme brutality of which human beings are capable, regardless of ethnicity, creed, or color. Racism undoubtedly was a factor in the execution of several black men when there was little evidence that they were guilty. In other instances, both black and white defendants were individuals of extreme brutality.

A few months following his appointment as chaplain, my father persuaded the governor to spare the life of James Dunmore, a nineteen-year-old black man from Georgetown County who had been accused of assault with intent to ravish a young white woman and condemned to death. Dunmore's sentence was commuted to life in prison, and there is no chapter on him. Created from my memory and news accounts from *The Columbia Record* and *The Charleston News and Courier,* the following paragraphs relate James Dunmore's narrow escape from the electric chair. The situation with James Dunmore quite forcefully illustrates the societal conditions of the 1940s and is included for that reason.

Chaplain Kelly Pleads for Governor Johnston to Spare the Life of James Dunmore

IT WAS MID-AFTERNOON ON Thursday, July 8, 1943, when James Dunmore sat for the second time to have his head shaved in preparation for his execution the next morning. Once previously, on January 7 of that same year, and with less than twenty-four hours to live, his head had been shaved in preparation for his execution the next morning. As one of his final acts, outgoing Governor R.M. Jefferies, granted a last minute, six-month stay of execution for James Dunmore.

The almost certainly innocent youth was again getting very close to his final hour on that July afternoon when Dad went to visit him. During their conversation, Dunmore looked the preacher straight in the eye and convinced him that he was not guilty. My father then rushed to the governor's office where his secretary informed him that the governor was ready to leave and he could not be seen before the next morning, which would have been too late for James Dunmore. However, Governor Johnston heard the conversation, came out of his office, and invited the chaplain to come in, even though he was hurrying to leave. Dad explained why he felt Dunmore was innocent and told the governor that he would stake his reputation as a judge of human character that young James Dunmore was being truthful. Dad explained that Dunmore did not deny knowing the girl. Nor, according to him, had he ever attempted to have sex with her. Dunmore told my father that he had been involved in an altercation with the girl's brother, his childhood friend who was also the landowner's son on the large farm where they all lived. And as a result of his getting the better of the white youth during some friendly roughhousing that had gotten heated, the youth's sister, in retaliation, claimed Dunmore had attempted to rape her. Governor Johnston issued a six-month stay of execution to study the case, and five months later, in December of 1943, Johnston commuted James Dunmore's sentence to life in prison.

Ironically, Governor Jefferies had granted the first six-month stay of execution back in January because of appeals for him to commute the sentence. *The Charleston News and Courier* reported on December 19, 1943, the day after the sentence had been commuted to life, that former Governor Jefferies had, in his reprieve order of the previous January, quoted from a letter by special trial Judge N.W. Eden, which said, in part: "...Descriptive conflict, the absence of corroborating circumstances, and subsequent developments are strongly indicative of factual error and I urge commutation of the sentence."

The jury foreman, name withheld, was quoted by Jefferies as writing, in part: "I am of the opinion Dunmore should have his sentence commuted to life... The testimony of the prosecuting witness was not clear and convincing."

Jefferies also quoted a telegraphed statement from a brother of the prosecuting witness: "I respectfully recommend commutation of James Dunmore's sentence because I am not convinced that he is the guilty man."

Had there been no open-door policy under Johnston, James Dunmore, an impoverished, third-grade dropout, would have died quite unjustly as another victim of the prevailing conditions that were a part of society during the 1940s. It was my father's firm conviction that James Dunmore was not guilty of any crime, let alone attempted rape, that helped to save Dunmore's life. Even so, Dunmore received a life sentence. James Dunmore was a model prisoner and guard Captain Frank Wilkes termed him a "good boy." Wilkes also quoted Dunmore as saying he was "too grateful not to die" to make any plans for seeking a new trial. It is my belief, though I have not been able to confirm it, that the charges against James Dunmore were dropped and his freedom was restored in 1944.

Several unsuccessful attempts were made to contact James Dunmore during the research of this book. If he is still alive, he is in his late eighties.

About the Governors

IT SHOULD BE NOTED that Governor Johnston, quite unlike most governors, would sometimes pay personal visits or send representatives to talk with doomed inmates just days before their appointment with the executioner. He wanted to hear their stories and determine if there was any justifiable reason to commute their sentences to life in prison.

Two years into his four-year term as governor, Johnston ran for and was elected to the U.S. Senate. There, in that august body, he served the people of South Carolina until his death over a quarter century later.

Johnston was succeeded by Lieutenant Governor Ransome J. Williams, who served out the remainder of the Johnston term. But Williams would lose his bid for re-election to Judge J. Strom Thurmond. From governor, Thurmond would go on to record his name on the pages of history in both South Carolina and Washington as a United States senator.

Governor Williams was himself a man of decency and integrity but not as accessible to my father as had been Governor Johnston. Nonetheless, Williams was diligent in his efforts to make certain that no innocent person was executed while he served as the state's chief executive. Williams once made the statement when an execution was pending: "I would rather commute the sentences of ten people who are guilty than to send one innocent person to his death."

Both Williams and Johnston were considered by some to be guilty of flawed reasoning for not intervening in several controversial cases and their reluctance to act would certainly be challenged when applying today's standards for capital punishment. However, neither of the governors desired to impose the death sentence. My father thought the two governors to be well ahead of their time when dealing with crime and punishment.

Dad served approximately seven months under Governor J. Strom Thurmond, after his inauguration to the office in January 1947. My father never met Thurmond until after his retirement from the ministry and his subsequent move back to his native South Carolina. However, Thurmond gave my father a thirty-day notice that he was terminated as of September 1, 1947, ostensibly to transition the chaplain's duties to a full-time responsibility. I decline to speculate here on Thurmond's motives.

Witness to Thirty-four Executions

INCLUDING THE ELECTROCUTION OF the Evans brothers in Chapter 1, who were executed before he became chaplain, my father witnessed a total of thirty-four deaths in either the electric chair or the gas chamber. However, he died holding firm his belief that capital punishment did not deter violent crime. He believed that the punishment one might receive is not contemplated when rage and emotion are involved. He was convinced that barroom brawls, street fights, and spontaneous acts of aggression, often the deeds of those with below normal intelligence, were beyond the scope of capital punishment as a deterring factor. He did feel, though, that the hardened criminal was swayed by the threat of capital punishment.

The hardest cases for my father to comprehend were crimes of revenge. He understood that spontaneous or vengeance-related murder could not go unpunished. Nonetheless, he was never convinced that the threat of death was a deterrent to such crimes.

He learned through experience that spontaneous homicides were often committed by people who were far more sensitive than were those heartless individuals who would deliberately burglarize homes, steal cars, rob banks, or commit other acts of violence.

It is my belief that my father's death house experiences offer a somewhat different and enlightening perspective on the subject of capital punishment than is usually understood by the general public. These stories of long-ago crimes and executions are my attempt to put capital punishment as it was practiced in the 1940s into perspective.

Chapter 1
The Evans Brothers

My father witnessed his first executions in South Carolina's electric chair on February 7, 1941, some two years before Governor Olin D. Johnston appointed him to serve as chaplain of the South Carolina state penitentiary and prisons system.

At the time the Evans brothers were put to death, Dad had no idea that he would become chaplain for the state's correctional institutions and that during his almost five years in that position he would witness the deaths of an additional twenty-nine men and three women.

Dad was accompanied to the Evans brothers' execution by the Reverend Charles F. Wimberly, a retired Methodist minister. In retirement, Wimberly served simultaneously as chaplain of the South Carolina Senate and as director of the Oliver Gospel Rescue Mission in downtown Columbia. The mission was a Methodist-sponsored ministry where my father often assisted as a volunteer. Its prime function was to offer spiritual counseling, a simple meal and a dormitory cot on which to sleep for the homeless men who came seeking refuge from the streets.

The jobless Evans siblings and the homeless drifters who sought sustenance and shelter at the rescue mission personified the societal problems related to the hardships of the times and of the Depression era. The clerics felt that by observing the angst of the brothers as they were put to death, they could better understand and counsel the young vagrants who came into their sphere of influence. Their goal was to prevent their mission-related contacts from drifting into very serious trouble, as had the Evans siblings.

The Evans Brothers' Crime

THE VICTIMS WERE PARKED in a lovers' lane near the confluence of the Broad and Saluda rivers where they join together to form the beautiful Congaree River just north of downtown Columbia. The isolated locale was popular among the few young people who had access to cars, and no other vehicles were seemingly in the area on the night of the assault. Perhaps the unsuspecting couple sat snuggled in the car enjoying the soft strains of some big band music on the radio, or perhaps they were merely conversing with each other. Nonetheless, the tranquility of that late summer evening in 1940 would end abruptly when the unarmed Hugh and Willis Evans and their cousin Hampton Lee converged on the auto and ordered the couple out of the car.

The trio then kicked and pummeled the young man with their fists before trying him up and taking turns raping his girlfriend. Bound and unable to intervene, he could do nothing but watch as the thugs repeatedly assaulted her.

The young woman was allegedly brutalized in numerous ways and bitten savagely on the breasts. It was rumored that an arresting officer, who was patrolling the area and just happened upon the ugly scene, asked, "What happened?" One of the culprits responded gleefully, "That is where I bit her."

The officer reportedly recoiled in anger and disgust and, some decades before the Miranda warning, used his fists to pound a measure of contrition into the head of the boastful culprit.

The Trial and Sentencing

THE CASE WAS TRIED in December 1940, and without doubt as to the identity of the offenders, who were all arrested at the scene of the crime, the jury deliberated quite briefly before returning a verdict of guilty against Hugh and Willis Evans and Hampton Lee. The judge passed the mandatory sentence of death and set the date of February 7, 1941, as the morning on which the three men would pay with their lives for the cruel violation of the innocent young woman. The sentence was not appealed, and they died on that day as sentenced.

Execution Day

THE COLUMBIA RECORD REPORTED the executions in its afternoon edition dated February 7, 1941. Following are excerpts from that article by reporter Eddie Finlay:

> Three Richland County farm boys and a Pickens County textile worker died in the electric chair at the state penitentiary this morning, the second largest execution of white men in the history of the state. Thirty-three minutes after the first man had entered the death chamber the last man had been pronounced dead.
>
> The four and the order in which they died were: Hugh Evans, 22: Willis Evans, 20, and Hampton Lee, 26, all of Richland County, and J. C. Hann, 27, of Pickens County.
>
> A considerable crowd had gathered in the drizzling rain outside the main gate to the prison by 6 o'clock, half an hour before the executions were scheduled to begin, and the witnesses trooped around to the death house in a chilly fog. Prisoners

3

peered down from lighted slits of windows in the main cell block and could be seen looking down through the open windows to the death house as the crowd gathered inside.

Hugh Evans, a slight, impassive faced man was the first to enter the death chamber, walking in calmly at exactly 6:30. Witnesses were lined up along the rail and five ministers who had spent many hours with the condemned men were seated on a little bench just behind.

As Evans stepped up into the chair the Rev. J. Wilson Lockwood, Baptist preacher of Columbia, began reading the 23rd Psalm. The condemned man, who leaves behind a wife, parents and several brothers and sisters, stared steadily at the blank wall, just above the heads of the spectators, raising his eyes slightly as the minister intoned, "The Lord is my shepherd."

Asked whether he had any last statement to make he said in a calm, low voice, "I am sorry for the things I've done. I accept the Lord as my savior. I am ready to go and meet my Savior."

He was pronounced dead three minutes and 39 seconds after the current was applied by State Electrician Sam Cannon. The prison physician, Dr. M. Whitfield Cheatham, was assisted by Dr. P.E. Payne and Dr. George K. Nelson.

Hugh Evans' 20-year old brother, Willis, also entered calmly but with eyes half closed and arms folded as he stepped up into the chair. A slightly sullen expression was on his face as he was asked by Capt. C.A. Sullivan whether he had any last statement to make.

"The Lord Jesus Christ has saved me," he said. "I am ready to go to the other place. I hope to see every one of you people there."

He was pronounced dead three minutes and 24 seconds later and there was a slight intermission as most of the witnesses walked out to make room for another group. Two women, however, stayed for the entire proceedings.

Hampton Lee, a tall, gangling man whose defense at his trial had been that he was feeble-minded, entered the chamber as the Rev. Lockwood read: "We have all sinned and come short of the glory of God."

He was calm and looked curiously around the room at the spectators as the straps were arranged.

"No, sir, I haven't nothing to say," he answered as Capt. Sullivan asked for his final statement. "Cept I hope you will be with me at a better place. I haven't saw them rings." (This was a reference to several valuable rings which were missing since the crime for which he was executed.)

He was pronounced dead three minutes and 31 seconds later and his body carried out into the little side room by prisoners assigned to the task.

Hann, a gaunt faced textile worker from Easley, also showed no emotion as he entered and kept his eyes turned toward the ceiling as the minister read.

"I want to look you good people straight in the face," he said, "and tell you I have made my peace with God. I thank Jesus for forgiving me. I am sorry for the crime I committed. I will meet you all in the morning." He was pronounced dead four minutes and 13 seconds later.

J. C. Hann Also Executed For Murder

THE TWENTY-SEVEN-YEAR-OLD HANN, A textile mill worker from the upstate town of Easley, was executed for the murder of Ruby Bolling in June of 1939. He was tried in September of that same year and was sentenced to die in February of 1940. However, his lawyers appealed the sentence to the state Supreme Court and his execution was stayed until February 7, 1941.

On the morning of the murder, Hann made an early morning call at the home of the twenty-eight-year-old Bolling, a young woman with whom he was familiar. She answered his knock and the two went out into the yard to talk. Moments later, Bolling's mother, who lived in the same house, heard her scream and rushed from the home to check on her daughter. The mother testified that: "Just as I reached the porch, I spotted J. C. holding Ruby with his left hand and using his right hand to slash her throat with a straight razor." As Bolling lay dying on the ground, her mother said, "I saw J. C. Hann hang the razor on a nearby rosebush and walk from the yard shaking my daughter's blood from his hands." For that act of premeditated murder, the State of South Carolina demanded the life of J. C. Hann.

Events Leading Up to Execution Day

THERE WAS BUT LITTLE news coverage of the rape of the Columbia woman, even though the crime was committed in the city's northern suburbs, and because of the limited press and media attention, rumors ran rampant. Many of the allegations were perhaps exaggerated, but they served to stir public outrage, and since there were no official denials, the public clamored to see the brothers and their cousin executed. There was not enough space in the execution chamber to accommodate all who wanted to attend. However, *The Columbia Record* reported that the prison superintendent, in response to public demand to witness the executions, had devised a plan to let one group of observers view the execution of the Evans brothers following which the execution chamber would be cleared and a second group would then be let into the grim little room to view Hampton Lee and J. C. Hann as they were put to death.

For reasons not revealed, two unidentified young women were allowed to view each of the four executions.

The men were all baptized the day before their executions and each individual spent time with various members of the clergy during the afternoon before their deaths. Among the ministers who visited the men was the penitentiary chaplain, the Reverend Mr. Z. P. Hamilton. All four youths died expressing remorse for their crimes, and each of them declared they were at peace with their Maker and were prepared to pay for their brutality.

The three men from Columbia were visited several times by relatives during their final week, and J. C. Hann's father and brother came down from Pickens County to visit with him for a few hours on Thursday.

Hampton Lee's mother visited him daily in the death house, and she walked the considerable distance from her home in the midtown area to spend time with her doomed son.

She probably had no means of transportation and could ill afford the cab or bus fare for a ride to the prison. Even so, she refused to abandon her errant child.

The Evans Brothers' Father

FOLLOWING THE EXECUTION OF the siblings, my father and the Reverend Wimberly went to search for the Evans family home in the suburbs east of Columbia.

They found the elderly father standing on his porch. They noted that he was a gray-haired gentleman who was slightly stooped and that his countenance was pained and saddened as he greeted these ministers, who were strangers to him.

The ministers did not tell him they had witnessed the executions and that his boys were gone. They introduced themselves as clerics and asked if they could read a few Bible verses and pray that God would grant him comfort. He seemed pleased to hear the scriptural passages, and he asked them to pray that he would receive strength and understanding. The old man thanked my father and Wimberly for their visit, but as the ministers were preparing to leave, he lost control of his emotions, and he clutched my father for support while sobbing bitterly.

Upon regaining his composure, the old gentleman said that his sons had been good lads but they had started drifting into trouble several years before the rape occurred. He related that the boys had occasionally gotten into some petty mischief but that nothing prior to the assault was of a very serious nature. Nonetheless, he acknowledged that from those first trivial infractions, the offenses became progressively worse until they terminated with the brutal violation of the blameless woman. And even as he mourned the loss of his sons, the elderly father expressed heartfelt concern for the young victim.

The miserable old man inquired if the ministers had word of the executions and, upon learning that his sons had already been put to death, he lowered his head and sobbed.

The old man's heartbreak inspired my father to use him as a sermon topic at many church venues. Dad related how that the actions of the sons had brought intense pain and suffering, not only to their own families, but also to their victims and their loved ones. Dad stressed that, once the perpetrators took their seats in the chair, their pain and suffering was soon over. However, for those left behind, the agony would never end.

The final paragraph in *The Columbia Record* article stated: "The largest previous execution of white men in the state occurred on March 24, 1939, when six convicts were electrocuted for the prison break slaying of Guard Captain J. Olin Sanders."

Archived records also reveal that six "Negro" inmates from Lexington County were executed on the same day in 1931.

Chapter 2
The Infamous Logue Story

On the frigid Thursday evening of January 14, 1943, my father nervously devoured a light supper, prayed with the family, and left the modest church parsonage to go and stay the night in the death house at the South Carolina state penitentiary. His mission was to spend the night with three condemned inmates who were awaiting execution at around seven o'clock the following morning. The executions would be his first official death chamber functions since becoming chaplain for the prisoners some two weeks prior. The time of execution, as with all electrocutions in South Carolina, would be on a Friday morning just about sunrise.

On that particular Thursday evening, my father followed the examples of some of his predecessors wherein he and several clergy colleagues spent the night with the condemned inmates who desired company during their final hours. However, most of those awaiting execution opted to spend their closing hours without visitors.

Individuals who had defiantly maintained their innocence, upon realizing there was no escaping the chair, sometimes came clean and confessed their guilt during those waning hours. Still others revealed unknown aspects of their crimes as the night ticked away. However, some withheld their confessions until just before leaving their cells to enter the execution chamber. The most stubborn and resolute waited until they sat strapped in the chair before confessing their guilt.

That mid-January morning in 1943 was, however, different from the usual routine for executions. For the first time since its installation, during the summer of 1912, a woman, Sue Logue, would die in South Carolina's electric chair.

The strong-willed Sue Logue, forty-three, came from a prominent family of farmers and landowners in rural Edgefield County. She was an elementary school teacher before she took part in a homicidal rampage that erupted in a dispute over three dollars. That trivial sum would ultimately cause the deaths of eight human beings. Five of those people died from gunshots and the other three from state-imposed electrocution. Additionally, Joe Frank Logue, the nephew of Sue Logue's slain husband, Wallace, would come within seven hours of taking his seat in the chair some thirteen months after the executions of his Aunt Sue, Uncle George, and a binge drinking rowdy named Clarence Bagwell.

The killing frenzy for which Bagwell and George and Sue Logue paid with their lives began almost two and a half years prior to their executions, in August of 1940, when a farm mule belonging to Davis Timmerman, a respected school board member in the district where Sue Logue had taught, escaped from the Timmerman side of adjoining pastures and delivered a deadly kick to the head of a calf belonging to Sue and Wallace Logue. Only a few strands of barbed wire separated the grazing animals, and no one ever knew exactly what provoked the mule to kick the yearling bull. Many believed the mule responded to a charge by the calf and, from that moment on, things spun insanely out of control.

On September 20, several weeks after the episode between the mule and the calf, Wallace Logue went to the general store owned by Davis Timmerman to collect payment for the prized Hereford. There, inside the store, the two men exchanged angry words over some pre-existing bad blood before they began negotiating the value of the young bull. They argued over the worth of the calf before ultimately concluding that fourteen dollars was sufficient, a sum that Timmerman paid immediately to Wallace Logue in cash. They shook hands and both considered the matter closed as Logue departed the store.

The Deadly Feud Escalates

WALLACE LOGUE RETURNED HOME to tell his wife that he had accepted a settlement. She argued that fourteen dollars was not a sufficient sum for the purebred calf, and she prevailed upon him to return to the store to demand an additional three dollars from Timmerman. Logue, at the insistence of his spouse, grudgingly returned to the rural retailer and pressured the storekeeper for more money.

Logue outweighed the slightly built Timmerman by some fifty or more pounds, and he was not pleased when the storeowner insisted that a deal was a deal and refused to pay more. Neither did he relish returning home to his temperamental wife without the additional dollars she had sent him to collect. Tempers flared, and Logue grabbed an axe handle from a nearby display. He seized Timmerman by the shirt and threatened him. In response, Timmerman retrieved a handgun from behind the service counter, and he shot and killed his attacker.

About five months later, Timmerman stood trial in March of 1941 for the murder of Wallace Logue. An Edgefield County jury found that the storeowner had acted in self-defense and acquitted him. However, immediately after learning the jury's verdict, Sue Logue allegedly confronted Sheriff L. H. Harling outside the courthouse and declared that if the people of Edgefield County would not punish Timmerman for killing her husband, she was prepared to take matters into her own hands.

Sue Logue and her brother-in-law, George Logue, a World War I army veteran and lifelong bachelor who lived in the family's plantation-style home along with his sister-in-law and his elderly mother, did not react immediately to the acquittal of Davis Timmerman. Instead, the outraged pair seethed quietly for several months and planned their revenge.

The Recruitment of Joe Frank Logue

GEORGE AND SUE LOGUE'S first action in their scheme to avenge Wallace Logue's slaying began with a visit to their nephew, Joe Frank Logue. The tall, dark haired and handsome Joe Frank Logue was a highly regarded police officer in the upstate city of Spartanburg where he had earned several awards for his work in law enforcement. Because he was bright, courteous, and friendly, many people assumed he would one day be Spartanburg's chief of police. Sue and George Logue demanded that he use his connections around Spartanburg to find someone to slay Timmerman.

Sue, Wallace, George, and other members of the Logue family had provided a good measure of support for Joe Frank and his younger siblings following the death of their own father, Joe Frank Logue Sr., in 1924, and he felt obligated to them. Sue and George Logue offered two hundred and fifty dollars each, a total of five hundred dollars, as payment to anyone who would kill Timmerman.

Joe Frank Logue tried to talk his aunt and uncle out of their plan, and he attempted to stall them, hoping they would not follow through, but this only made them angry, and they returned to Spartanburg to remind him of his obligation to them and demand action. Joe Frank Logue told my father this story:

> Sue and George Logue, during their second visit, insinuated that bad things would happen to his wife or his mother if he failed to comply with their demand to find someone to snuff out the life of Davis Timmerman. Joe Frank Logue told that he was all too aware of the Logue family's reputation

to get what they wanted or of the consequences that would ensue for anyone who did not accede to their demands. He declared that if someone refused to sell a horse, a dog or other property that certain members of the family coveted, the horse would become lame, the dog would die, and the other properties destroyed or rendered useless.

Whether Joe Frank Logue's version of the Logue family reputation had merit or was unfounded, he repeatedly told my father: "I feared what would happen to my wife or my mother if I did not comply with my aunt and uncle's demand to hire someone to murder Timmerman."

Joe Frank Logue Hires the Gunman

JOE FRANK LOGUE KNEW of Clarence Bagwell, a local rowdy who had allegedly declared that he would kill everyone in Spartanburg County for five hundred dollars. Joe Frank Logue contacted Bagwell and asked if he meant what he said when he made the boast. Bagwell, a nice looking ladies' man of stocky build, was in his early thirties and notorious around the area as a barroom brawler. He responded that he had once boasted: "As broke as I am, I will kill everyone in Spartanburg County for five hundred dollars, but I said it while drunk and did not mean it."

Joe Frank Logue knew that Bagwell was an alcoholic, and he began furnishing him with the liquor he craved. As Bagwell swilled, Logue kept increasing the pressure on him to kill the storekeeper, and after days of virtually non-stop drinking, Bagwell consented. Logue quickly scheduled a day off and arranged for a fellow officer to cover his duties while he drove Bagwell to Edgefield County to make the hit on the storekeeper.

Joe Frank Logue knew that someone might recognize his car in the Meeting Street area where the crime was to be committed, so he borrowed the car of a friend. En route to Edgefield County,

Bagwell continued to sip from a bottle of whiskey, and he later stated that Logue consumed his share of whiskey on the trip. However, Logue denied drinking.

Upon arriving in Edgefield and before heading out to the Timmerman place of business, Logue moved to the back seat and concealed himself under a raincoat. Bagwell drove to the gas pump in front of the store, and the unsuspecting Timmerman came out to pump the gas. When he was finished at the pump, Bagwell got directions into town and paid for the gas, after which Timmerman went back into the store.

As Bagwell steered away from the gasoline pump, Logue identified the man who had pumped the gas as the person they were there to kill.

Timmerman's wife was inside the store and had gotten a glimpse of Bagwell as he drove away. Before she left the store and walked across the road to their home, she testified later, her husband observed that the car had taken the opposite direction from the instructions he had given them for the route into Edgefield.

Davis Timmerman is shot

BAGWELL DROVE A FEW miles away from town before turning back to the store. With Joe Frank Logue still hiding in the back seat, Bagwell parked at the gas pump and left the motor idling while he went inside. He asked for a pack of cigarettes, and as Timmerman turned to pull the pack from behind the counter, Bagwell pulled his gun and said, "Turn around. I am going to kill you, but I will not shoot a man in the back." As the storekeeper turned to face him, Bagwell emptied the revolver of its six bullets, five of which hit their mark. He then ran to the car and drove back to Spartanburg. Logue returned to his duties as a police officer the next morning.

The killers left no fingerprints or circumstantial evidence, and there were no eyewitnesses to connect them to the shooting.

Bagwell's conscience bothered him, though, and he used the five hundred dollars he received to fund a new round of drinking.

While he was drunk, Bagwell told a female companion that he knew the details of the recent shooting down in Edgefield. The young woman remembered reading of the murder and worried that she might be implicated somehow if she did not go to the authorities. The frightened young woman went to the police and told them of Bagwell's drunken boast.

Police immediately took Bagwell into custody, and after several hours of intense grilling, he confessed to killing Timmerman. Bagwell identified Joe Frank Logue as the man who hired him and as the person who accompanied him to the scene of the shooting. The interrogators compared the date of the murder with the date Logue had taken off from his patrol duties, and the dates coincided.

The authorities then asked Joe Frank Logue to come voluntarily to police headquarters and answer some questions. Following a brief interrogation by his fellow officers, Logue was handcuffed and held for additional questioning. The Spartanburg authorities took him to the state penitentiary in Columbia, where a team of the state's expert examiners grilled him.

At the penitentiary, Logue went to a cell in the solitary confinement section that the guards and inmates knew as "Cuba." He endured endless hours of isolation, where the inmates subsisted on nothing but bread and water. Logue realized the awful mess he had made of his life. Recognizing his dire situation, he dropped to his knees and accepted Christ as his Savior. Then he called for the examiners. During a lengthy confession, he implicated Sue and George Logue as instigators of the plot, and he admitted he had plied Bagwell with liquor and coaxed him to do the murder.

With Wallace Logue and Davis Timmerman already dead and Clarence Bagwell, Joe Frank Logue, and George and Sue Logue facing indictment for murder, the quarrel over the calf should have been finished, but it would not end until three additional lives were lost to gunfire.

Following Joe Frank Logue's confession, Spartanburg authorities contacted the recently elected Edgefield County Sheriff W. D. "Wad" Allen to share what they had learned from Bagwell and Joe Frank Logue. Allen, known as a devout Christian and respected throughout the county, was a distant cousin of the Logues. Upon hearing the details of the confession, the sheriff contacted George and Sue Logue and asked that they come voluntarily to his office and tell him what they knew of the Timmerman murder. He received no response for two or three days. Sheriff Allen decided to drive out to the Logue homestead and have a conversation with them.

On a Sunday morning, November 16, 1941, the sheriff called his friend and deputy, W. L. "Doc" Clark, to go with him. The sheriff telephoned to inform the Logues that he had warrants for their arrest and that he was on his way.

Before he left his office, the sheriff undoubtedly had a premonition of death. He expressed his anxiety in a handwritten message left on his desk. The note read, "If I never return, I have served God and country to the best of my ability." Nevertheless, he did not strap on a gun. He seldom carried one.

Gun Battle at Logue Home

WHEN THEY PULLED UP to the home, the officers saw George Logue standing in the side yard. The sheriff explained his mission, and George Logue invited them to come inside. He instructed the officers to wait on the front porch as he went through a side entrance to open the front door for them. They waited until someone opened the door and invited them to come in. As the sheriff and his deputy stepped inside, they were cut down by a barrage of gunfire.

George and Sue Logue and a sharecropper, Fred Dorn, were all inside the room, and the two men were armed with a shotgun and a pistol. Sheriff Allen died instantly from a bullet fired from the pistol of George Logue, and Deputy Clark took a disemboweling blast from the shotgun of the sharecropper. Clark got off a shot of his own that critically wounded Dorn, who would die some hours later that night in a Greenwood hospital.

As the deputy lay dying on the front porch, he "was roll kicked" into the yard by a woman believed to be Sue Logue, he later reported. She supposedly told him, "Die in the yard like the dog that you are, not on my front porch."

Showing an incredible will to live, Deputy Clark managed to get out to the road and flag down a passing auto. The deputy related the events of the morning to the driver who sped him across the Savannah River to a hospital in Augusta, Georgia. Clark continued to talk in the emergency room, as doctors and nurses worked frantically to save him, but he died hours after he arrived at the hospital.

With the sheriff, the sharecropper, and the deputy all gunned down, the three-dollar feud that began in September of 1940 had caused the deaths of five human beings within a time span of just fourteen months. Even then, however, death refused to take a holiday.

Judge J. Strom Thurmond Becomes Involved

IMMEDIATELY FOLLOWING THE GUN battle, law enforcement officers rushed to the Logue property where they found George and Sue Logue barricaded inside. They refused to surrender, and following a lengthy standoff, an up-and-coming judge with a no-nonsense reputation arrived on the scene. Judge J. Strom Thurmond negotiated briefly with the pair before they reluctantly agreed to surrender. Thurmond offered them nothing but his personal guarantee for their safety and the promise they would receive a fair trial. Even with the judge's assurances, the Logues were afraid of the local authorities, and Thurmond agreed to accompany them and the arresting officers to the Lexington County jail.

At their pre-trial hearing, George and Sue Logue and Clarence Bagwell all felt, and it was argued by their lawyers, that they could not receive a fair trial in the county of Edgefield, and the attorneys requested a change in venue. News of the five killings had dominated the news in the Logues' home county for over a year, and they feared standing trial before an Edgefield County jury. After about five hours of debate between the defense attorneys and the prosecutor, Judge G. Duncan Bellinger granted the request for a change and moved the trial to Lexington County. Judge Bellinger also presided at the trial in Lexington County, which is located some fifty miles east of Edgefield. Nevertheless, George and Sue Logue and Clarence Bagwell were convicted and sentenced to death.

Joe Frank Logue preferred to stand trial in Edgefield County, and he said he would accept the punishment the citizens of Edgefield demanded of him. During the trial, Logue expressed remorse and answered questions truthfully, as he made his plea for mercy. The jury was not sympathetic and found him guilty. He was the fourth person in the case to be sentenced to death.

When my father spoke of the Logue/Timmerman feud, he often reflected on the pain, suffering, and senseless loss of human lives over "a bargain rate of three human lives for a dollar."

The Executions on January 15, 1943

SUE LOGUE WAS THE first of the trio executed on that cold January morning, and she would be the first of her gender put to death in the state's electric chair. She had spent a sleepless night in the company of a nurse who stayed inside the cell with her. The nurse did what she could to keep Sue Logue calm and comfortable, but throughout the long night, Sue Logue trembled and sometimes shook violently. My father said: "Sue lay cowered in the fetal position and was covered by a blanket throughout most of her final hours."

When her time came to die, Sue Logue, accompanied by several guards, walked un-assisted into the execution chamber and took her seat in the electric chair. The penal authorities didn't force her to wear her prison dress that day, and she entered the death chamber clad in gray slacks and a white blouse acquired specifically for her execution. Once she was seated, however, she could not be strapped in. The bindings were too lengthy for her small limbs, and a guard went hurriedly in search of a tool to punch additional holes in the thick leather straps. That glitch added some eight to ten minutes to her agonizing wait.

During those minutes that she sat in the chair unstrapped, she seemed calm, and she exchanged pleasantries with the guards who were standing by. My father admired her courage and the manner in which she faced her final moments. Finally, the restraints were adjusted properly. The executioner flipped a switch, and Sue Logue died in less than three minutes, which my father said was a mercifully short time. Typically, electrocutions required from three to a bit more than five minutes.

George Logue followed his sister-in-law into the execution chamber, and he made a lengthy and bitter final statement, a statement in which he accused others of telling lies that sent him to the chair. He vehemently denied the testimony against him, and he never admitted to taking part in the murder of Davis Timmerman. When he was done, he was electrocuted. Dr. M. Whitfield Cheatham, the attending physician, pronounced him dead after about four minutes, and George Logue became the seventh person to die because of the petty feud. He had revealed to my father during one of their death house conversations that he had once been a member of a tour group that visited the prison and, during the outing he sat in the electric chair as a joke. George Logue remarked that he had had no idea then that he would die in that chair. My father said that George Logue himself saw the irony in his own situation.

Clarence Bagwell was the last to be executed on that morning. As he entered the iron door into the execution compartment, he recoiled suddenly and was visibly startled to see prison trustees removing George's body through an exit doorway. However, he immediately regained his composure and resumed his walk to the chair.

Bagwell sat down and thanked the guards for treating him well. He said he was ready to go. My father asked about his relationship with the Almighty, to which Bagwell replied, "I have given my heart to Christ, and I am ready to meet my Savior." Just before the captain of the guard tapped his cane on the concrete floor, which was the signal for executioner Sam Cannon to throw the switch, Bagwell apologized for what he had done.

The Funerals

FOLLOWING THE EXECUTIONS, MY father and the Reverend Charles F. Wimberly drove to Edgefield and attended the joint funeral services for George and Sue Logue. At the service, they met the mother of George Logue. She had seen two of her sons, Joe Frank Sr., who was shot, and Wallace, lose their lives to violence. Then, on that afternoon, she was attending a funeral service for yet another of her sons in addition to her daughter-in-law Sue. However, even as the elderly Mrs. Logue grieved, her grandson, Joe Frank Logue Jr., languished in a cell at the nearby Edgefield County jail awaiting his own appointment with the executioner.

Her suffering devastated the pair of ministers, and they could barely control their emotions when she cried out, "How much more can I take? How much more must I endure? Please, God, take me." Mrs. Logue was a devoutly religious woman, and she had always been a respected wife, mother, and neighbor. Her godly influence was the reason that her grandson, Joe Frank Jr., had once contemplated becoming a Christian minister. His calling to the ministry was delayed for years while he served his time in prison.

Dad conducted worship services at his Church of the Nazarene in Columbia on the Sunday morning following the executions on Friday, and then he rushed off to Spartanburg to direct the memorial service for Clarence Bagwell. My father needed someone to go with him, and he chose me. I was eleven years old. Even though Dad and Bagwell had met for the first time in the death house nineteen days before the execution, they formed an immediate bond, and Bagwell asked my father to conduct the memorial service.

The undertaker claimed the body following the execution, but he didn't know the place and time for the funeral, only that the service was to be in Spartanburg on Sunday afternoon. He instructed Dad to get directions at a service station when Dad reached the outskirts of the city, about two hours north of Columbia.

A few miles south of Spartanburg, traffic slowed to a crawl as each car stopped for a few seconds before a South Carolina Highway Patrol officer motioned them to continue. When Dad got to the roadblock, the officer stated that he needed to escort my father to the Bagwell funeral. With his emergency lights flashing, the officer led Dad through downtown and out to a nightspot on the Asheville highway. Bagwell's wife had been unable to secure a church location for the funeral, and she had decided to hold it in the Green Gables Night Club, which she owned. The service was on the dance floor of the tavern and, in death, Bagwell returned to a place he loved.

The funeral home provided extra chairs, but still an overflow crowd spilled out into the parking area and along the highway. Against a wall at the edge of the dance floor, the body of Clarence Bagwell lay in its coffin. Even though prison authorities had cut his hair in preparation for electrocution, the mortician had skillfully attached much of the hair back to the scalp.

Signs throughout the nightspot were covered in black crepe paper, and in that unusual setting, my father conveyed the message that Bagwell had specifically requested of him, namely to tell his friends that he had accepted Christ as his Savior and that he wanted them to join him in heaven.

When the funeral sermon was finished, Dad gave an altar call on the nightclub's dance floor. He asked if anyone present would like to accept Christ as his or her Savior and to one day meet Bagwell in heaven. Everyone in the crowd bowed their heads and closed their eyes, and seventeen of Bagwell's old drinking friends raised their hands for prayer, and seven more came forward to kneel at the casket and pray.

From a religious standpoint, Dad felt that, considering the way things turned out, the tavern was not a bad place for the funeral. After talking with many individuals who were friends of Bagwell, Dad felt that many among them would have refrained from attending the service had it been within a church sanctuary. He felt, however, that in the Green Gables Night Club, Bagwell's rowdy friends were much more at ease.

Observations

MY FATHER OPENED HIS heart to the three murderers and had done his best to comfort and guide them spiritually during their final weeks of life. He gave them everything that he could give. However, only Clarence Bagwell responded. Bagwell was like an open book, my father said. He told Dad everything of his sordid past and the murder of Davis Timmerman. In addition, just before Bagwell left his cell on his way to the electric chair, he handed my father his small prayer booklet, an item that is still in possession of the Kelly family.

George and Sue Logue died without ever admitting guilt. Dad believed the closest he came to reaching either of them was on a day when George Logue looked at him through the bars and said, "Preacher, please pray for me." Dad said that George, who always looked strong and tough, wore the most pitiful expression Dad had ever witnessed, and he felt sorry for him.

Chapter 3
The Enigmatic Clarence Bagwell

After decades of wondering how and why the likable Clarence Bagwell could have gone so wrong, I decided to visit his hometown to search for answers. The Bagwells had, over a century and a half earlier, settled near the city of Brevard, North Carolina, a picturesque little town where the Main Street shops and restaurants and the quaint old courthouse seem to leap from the folios of early Americana.

Defining the city is Brevard College with its renowned school of music, which is widely recognized for its teaching program and the eclectic concerts that are featured on the campus. The upscale society stemming from the school transcends the condition of poverty that is common throughout much of Appalachia. Customs and traditions from an earlier time survive in the surrounding hills, and the area is known for its cool summers and blaze-colored autumns that draw tourists in droves.

Brevard is the seat of government for Transylvania County, an area where native Cherokee tribesmen fished the clear streams for brook trout and roamed the ridges and valleys in search of wild game, fruits, nuts and berries.

The Bagwells came when Scots and Irish settlers were pushing civilization ever westward across the continent and clearing land for farming. They were proud pioneers who were fiercely independent, and they tended to ignore unjust, or just inconvenient, laws. Many built stills and sampled freely from Mason jars filled with what they called "white lightning" or "moonshine."

The Bagwell clan was established in the region before the Civil War, and their men went off to fight. Family legend has it that, while the men were away battling for the Confederacy, Union soldiers harassed many of the women and raped at least one.

In those hills, a man's word was his bond, and business deals were sealed with a promise and a handshake.

Such were the conditions into which Clarence Bagwell was born in 1908 and nurtured.

In Search of the Real Clarence Bagwell

IT IS HARD TO fathom the enigma that was Clarence Bagwell. Webster's dictionary defines one of the meanings of enigma as "something that is a riddle or inexplicable." If ever such a definition applied to an individual man, it applied to Clarence, the hard drinking fellow who was well liked by nearly everyone who knew him. However, he was a self-willed young man who was ready and able to rumble on a moment's notice. He was a chap who accepted pay to commit a murder, but he was neither a thief nor a robber. He was a big hearted individual with impulsive instincts and he repented of his crime and begged forgiveness from God and his victim's family.

The story of Sue and George Logue has been fully explored and narrated during the seventy years since they and Bagwell were executed. However, no one has delved deeply into the background of Bagwell, the Logue's hired gunman who shot Davis Timmerman. This narrative is to provide insight into the complexities that defined the man the locals called "Buster."

In August of 2009, accompanied by Kim Kelly-Burton, my niece, I set out to learn what I could of Clarence Bagwell.

25

The first contact was with Marshall Loftis, who knew Bagwell from the time Loftis was a boy.

The second meeting was with the Reverend Billy Patterson, who did not know Bagwell personally. However, Patterson's father made a living selling moonshine whisky to Bagwell and his rowdy companions, and the reverend grew up hearing tales of Bagwell's exploits.

In addition to the interviews with Loftis and Patterson, my niece spoke to Bagwell's relatives still living in the area by phone or mail. Several Bagwell cousins who now live in other states and cities supplied family history and old photographs. Through such sources we learned that Bagwell's parents and some of the Bagwell children were devoutly religious and that he had a twin sister named Callie. Callie died when she was hit by a car. Her granddaughter said Callie went to her grave believing that Bagwell was framed and that he was incapable of committing murder.

The guilt of Bagwell, however, is beyond any doubt. He and Joe Frank Logue, a Spartanburg police officer, both confessed to their involvement in the shooting of Davis Timmerman. And on the night before his execution, Bagwell confirmed his guilt to my father and other clergymen.

During that final night, Bagwell also voiced his concern that Joe Frank Logue, the man who swayed him to commit murder, would never be executed. Even though Logue was under a sentence of death, Bagwell was adamant that he would not die in the chair. Dad explained that Logue was regarded as the most contemptible of the group and that, with public sentiment running so strongly against him, he would be unable to escape the deadly consequences of his actions. However, some thirteen months following that conversation, Bagwell's concerns would prove prophetic when Governor Olin D. Johnston went to the death house at midnight to commute Logue's sentence.

Bagwell Looks Forward to Breakfast in Heaven

CLARENCE TOLD MY FATHER and his associates that he was thankful for the electric chair. The following is excerpted from Dad's handwritten notes:

> They were brought to the death house on Christmas day, this was 1942. I went to see them the next day and they all professed to have been saved and were ready to die. George and Sue never made a full confession of their guilt or of having any part in the crime—we visited them almost daily until their time came to die—we spent the night in the death house. Bagwell said "I thank God for the electric chair, had I been killed on the street, I would have been lost, but now I'm saved, and I'm going to have breakfast with Jesus tomorrow."

The individuals interviewed and the Bagwell kin who provided photos and information were firm in their opinion that the Bagwell family were responsible citizens and well liked throughout the area. They went about their business and did not cause trouble. Thus, Clarence Bagwell defied his upbringing when he killed Timmerman, a murder that netted him five hundred dollars and death in the chair.

The Interviews

LOFTIS REMEMBERED THAT BAGWELL came frequently to his home to drink moonshine with his father. The warm and personable Loftis, now in his mid-eighties and a decorated veteran of World War II, had only good things to say about his dad's old hooch-swilling partner. He concurred with my father's description of Bagwell, that he was a happy-go-lucky individual who epitomized the meaning of the phrase: "What you see is what you get."

"Buster was not a mean person, nor did I think of him as having the mindset of a criminal," Loftis said. "He was a dare-devil personality, an individual who would not back away from a fight. He would accept any challenge thrown at him."

To add emphasis to Dad's description of the reckless Bagwell personality, the following excerpt is from my father's handwritten notes:

> Joe had heard of a young man, Clarence Bagwell, who had made a statement that he would kill everyone in the county for $500. He was married to a woman who owned the Green Gables night club on the Spartanburg Hendersonville Highway—when Joe approached Clarence about his statement, He said, "O—I didn't mean that—I couldn't kill everyone in the county—Joe said, "You don't have to. I can get you five hundred to kill just one man, and you don't need to think of it as being murder, it will be like killing a dog." (The fact is that Mr. Timmerman was a respected farmer, a store keeper and a member of the school board.) Clarence had made a foolish vow and now to save face he found it hard to back down. Clarence became interested and Joe took him to see Sue and George—Clarence told me that he was not a murderer at heart and in order to bolster his nerves, the Logues furnished him with all the whiskey he could drink for several weeks.

Marshall Loftis provided even more proof of the dare-devil personality of Bagwell. He stated that back during the 1930s, a touring circus had visited Brevard. The circus had a highly touted "strongman" and would pay five dollars, the equivalent of a week's wages during those early years of the Great Depression, to anyone who could last three rounds in the boxing ring with their man, Loftis said. Bagwell, whose fists earned him a short term in prison for manslaughter prior to the Timmerman murder, was up to the challenge. Not only did Bagwell last the required three rounds in the ring, he beat the circus strongman soundly.

But Bagwell had a gentle side, too, Loftis said, and he illustrated this point with another anecdote: During one of Bagwell's drinking sessions with Marshall Loftis' father, Bagwell had called Loftis, then seven or eight, to come over and sit on his knee. Bagwell wanted to show him a pocketknife he had just purchased. The boy expressed delight, and Bagwell handed him the knife and told him to keep it.

During our interview, Loftis did not mention his Navy service, but as we left his home, we saw a framed display of military ribbons and medals. Only then did he reveal that he was a decorated veteran of World War II and that he served in the Pacific Theater of Operations. We invited him to lunch, but he declined, explaining that he was about to leave for a nursing home, where he went every day to feed his wife of many decades her lunch.

The Reverend Billy Patterson

OUR INTERVIEW WITH THE Reverend Billy Patterson came over an enjoyable lunch in a locally owned restaurant on Main Street. The retired cleric accepted the invitation to dine and share his father's stories of Clarence Bagwell. He told us that Bagwell was a frequent visitor at his parents' home, where he would come to purchase the moonshine for which the elder Patterson was locally famous. Once, when Bagwell and a young female companion came for a half gallon jar of liquor, he said, Bagwell opened the jar on his way back to the car and stopped to take a swig. The bottle had barely touched his lips when a frightening clap of thunder sounded and a streak of lightning flashed low across the sky. Everyone stood still, shaken—everyone except Bagwell, who raised the jar toward heaven and challenged, "You SOB, do it again!"

Despite his father's illegal occupation, Billy Patterson went on to study theology and be ordained as a Baptist minister, in much the same manner as did another son of a bootlegger, the Reverend Jerry Falwell. And like Falwell, Patterson returned to his hometown to pastor a church among the peers of his youth. Patterson's boyhood friends, as well as the parents and relatives of Clarence Bagwell, were numbered among those in his church congregation. Despite his long association with the Bagwells, the reverend could not explain the enigma that was Clarence Bagwell, but he concurs with the widespread opinion that the Bagwells are a decent, law-abiding family.

Other longtime residents of Brevard and members of the Bagwell family told stories and recounted rumors that could not be substantiated, but one is worth repeating here, if only to show how Bagwell is remembered in his hometown. It is a well-established fact that Bagwell was a brawler, and rumor has it that he once bit off a man's finger in a fistfight.

People around Brevard still talk about Bagwell's funeral where, one person said, "Buster's casket was placed atop the bar in the Green Gables Night Club, and his wife and friends danced and partied the night away around the coffin." As a boy of about eleven, I attended the Bagwell funeral, and I have my doubts. Mrs. Bagwell, also known as Mrs. Smith, was a large woman who was ten or more years her husband's senior. As I remember it, she wept softly and dabbed her eyes throughout the funeral. Even had she been in a festive mood, I don't believe that she would have denigrated her husband's Christian conversion by sponsoring such a party, and such a party would have violated South Carolina's blue laws, which prohibited drinking in a public place from midnight on Saturday through midnight on Sunday. The funeral did attract an overflow crowd to the tavern that Sunday, though, and stalled traffic a half mile in each direction.

At the end of my father's funeral sermon, seven of Bagwell's old friends came up to pray for salvation.

Authors Note: Marshall Loftis passed away following our interview and we were saddened to learn of his passing. The time spent with him was informative and enjoyable.

Chapter 4
The Mentally Challenged Jesse Jones

The murder of J. L. Hughes, a respected sixty-nine-year-old farmer from the Glendale area of Spartanburg County, and the subsequent indictment, conviction, and execution of the mentally deficient black youth, Jesse Jones, was one of the more bizarre situations in which my father was involved during his years as chaplain at the penitentiary. Jones was twenty at the time of his execution on April 2, 1943. The case against Jones involved the ax murders of four elderly people.

Archived records at the South Carolina State Supreme Court library and old news reports by *The Spartanburg Herald* reveal that Jones was tried and convicted only for the murder of J. L. Hughes, even though he was indicted for killing both Mr. and Mrs. Hughes on or about February 24, 1942. Jones was also indicted, but never tried, for the murders of Columbus Petrie, eighty-one, and his sister, Ida Petrie, who was seventy-nine. The Petries were hacked to death inside their home in the Ben Avon section of the county during a nighttime break-in that had occurred on February 14, ten days prior to the Hughes murders. The circumstances under which the two homes had been invaded and the four murders committed were virtually identical.

Additionally, a younger Petrie sister, Maggie, was brutally beaten and left for dead on the night that her brother and sister were slain. They had all been attacked inside the home where the three siblings lived. Maggie somehow survived, and after weeks of intensive care in a nearby hospital, she was allowed to return home.

The Hughes and Petrie residences were slightly more than a mile apart, and the murderer had entered through windows that were pried open. Once inside, he unscrewed the light bulbs from sockets suspended from the ceiling before seeking out his targets. He attacked them with an ax used to split wood. J. L. Hughes' skull was fractured in three places, and this was the murder for which Jesse Jones was twice tried and convicted. However, it is virtually certain that the diminutive Jones—who was just over five feet, six inches tall and weighed 127 pounds, according to his execution file at the state Department of Archives and History—killed all four victims and beat the surviving woman, as well. Jones was nineteen when the crimes took place.

Spartanburg County police worked diligently to garner evidence, which, though circumstantial, overwhelmingly established that Jones was the perpetrator. At the trial, investigating officers produced several bloodstained garments belonging to Jones that were found scattered along a railroad track a few miles from the scene of the Hughes murders. The items of apparel were traced back to Jones through a local merchant who attested that he had extended credit and sold the garments to the woman who was Jones' guardian and one of his regular customers.

Police also revealed that they had found the Hughes' pick-up truck that had been stolen on the night of the murders. The truck was empty of gas, and it had been left by the side of the road that ran adjacent to the railroad tracks, only a mile from where the bloody clothes were discovered. Jones denied taking the vehicle, and he repeatedly declared that he could not drive. He admitted to being at the scene of the slaying but denied having any part. He alleged that someone else had committed the murder and forced him to participate by putting him under a spell, which left him with no will of his own.

Jones was indicted for all four of the Hughes/Petrie murders, but Solicitor S. R. Watt decided to try him only for the killing of J. L. Hughes. Even though Jones was going on trial for his life, Judge M. M. Mann waited until Monday, April 20, 1942, less than three full days before his trial was to begin, to appoint Matthew Poliakoff, John Lanham, and R. B. Palsay Jr. to represent the indigent suspect.

Jones' short life had not been an easy one. When he was only weeks old, Jones' mother abandoned him and left him in the care of a woman who was said to be his grandmother. Nonetheless, on several occasions during the first of his one-day trials, Dolly Jones was referenced as his stepmother. Official records at the state penitentiary list Dolly Jones as his foster mother. Her relationship to the defendant was never fully established, but that impoverished woman nurtured and supported Jones from the time he was an infant, and she was the only authority figure he had ever known.

The Pre-trial Hearing

THE FIRST TRIAL FOR Jesse Jones began and ended on April 23, 1942, two months following the Hughes murder, and he was condemned to death. Due to the brevity of the trial and the inadequate time the appointed lawyers were allowed to devise their strategy, one might assume that Jones' attorneys were lax in their efforts to defend their client. Nothing could be further from the truth. Immediately following their appointment, the team of defenders went to work in a futile attempt to spare his life. Psychiatrists later determined that Jones had the mental capacity of a six-year-old.

On April 21, 1942, just the day following his appointment to the case, attorney John C. Lanham pleaded with Judge Mann to delay the trial until the July session of criminal court. Lanham, who was opposed by Solicitor Watt at the pre-trial hearing, argued vigorously for the judge to send his client to the state hospital in Columbia for thirty days to be examined and evaluated by qualified psychiatrists. Mann listened, though testily at times, to Lanham's pleas. However, the judge refused to postpone the proceedings and ordered that the trial begin in two days, as scheduled.

The following notes are excerpted from the Jones appeal before the Supreme Court, which contains 101 total pages. They are in reference to attorney Lanham's argument to postpone the trial. His argument was made before Judge Mann on April 21, 1942, two days before the trial began on the 23rd. The appeal transcripts are on file at the South Carolina Supreme Court library. Mann was sympathetic to a mental examination, but he was adamant that such an evaluation could be done in two days by local physicians who were not psychiatrists. The terms that Lanham used to describe his client are sometimes shocking, but I chose to leave them unedited, since they reveal the justice system as it was.

Attorney Lanham argued: "Every phase of this case and every circumstance, all the conditions connected with the case, as we have found them in our investigation, have been clearly reflective of the fact that this defendant is of a peculiar mental makeup. We are fully convinced that he is the victim of dementia praecox. That is the only question that we can conscientiously direct the Court's attention to. That is the only serious question."

Attorney Lanham was passionate as he continued his argument before Judge Mann. And even though he used the word "darkey" to describe his client, records show his intent was not to show disrespect for the black youth he was defending. He simply used the term because it was considered a polite way to avoid the use of the "N" word, which was common in that day.

Attorney Lanham continued:

It is a much greater tragedy to be mentally sick than to be physically unsound. My friend will say: "Well, it is a bad killing; there is too much killing."

We agree with him there. But that is not the point, sir. The point is whether this man is mentally ill or mentally normal. We know what the legal test is. We think the only fair thing to do is to allow this darkey to be sent for observation and examination for thirty (30) days, and let the authorities tell our jury what the result of that examination and observation is. I have communicated with Ethel Sharp, psychiatrist, to see if we could not have an expert here to give the jury the benefit of expert knowledge; she said she could not be here.

Dr. Beckham did not know whether he could be here today. He would not want to make only a cursory examination.

Now, this is a new case. There has been no unnecessary delay. The request, we think, is a very reasonable one, horrible! Exceptionally horrible, though the circumstances be! The people of the community, though they feel that they have been outraged, they are fair enough; they are broadminded enough to give this little black Negro his rights.

Far be it from us to want to put off this case. I have never been an attorney who nagged at the Solicitor's coat tail to delay the Court or to put off trials. Since we are receiving no compensation, we are even more concerned than if we were being paid. We came to the conclusion that we must not be concerned either personally or professionally but wholly governed by the desire that justice be done to both the state and to the defendant. Since Your Honor has had the confidence in us to place his interests in our hands, we feel that we owe this little darkey an obligation, which if not discharged conscientiously and sincerely, then we are not loyal to our duty.

I would like very much to see this case disposed of. If this darkey is sent down there and examined and observed, he will have the benefit of every consideration the Court and the law could extend to him. Whether you go to sit down and sizzle in the electric chair, or whether you spend the rest of your life in the penitentiary, everything that the law could do to protect you has been done. We have another term of criminal court in July. Personally, I would rather go ahead and try the case now. But that is not the question. It is not a question of what suits the Solicitor's convenience or our convenience; but what is our conscientious duty. The newspapers say that he blinked vigorously. It does not matter what the newspapers think or say. Your Honor saw him and his demeanor. Watching his gestures and his general manner there is enough evidence to conclude that this boy is not normal— there is enough to justify making this test. There is enough evidence sticking out there in patent view to make it the humane thing to do, even if he is not crazy enough to meet the test.

All we are asking is to have the opportunity to let them look him over and tell the jury what they think of him. They have the right to do that; and the jury has the right to hear their testimony; and then to say whether though it is bad killing this little Negro is a psychotic personality; he did not know right from wrong—he looks more like a monkey than he does a human being. They have the right to do that; and since they have, I believe this darkey ought to have the benefit of that chance; and we so move.

EXCHANGE BETWEEN LANHAM AND the Court Following Plea to Postpone the Trial

The Court: Yesterday afternoon, I gave you the authority of the Court to request medical examination of this defendant. Have any doctors agreed to do this? Have you complied with the Court's offer?

Mr. Lanham: We have been to see local physicians. They say that since this is a mental case we should have the opinion of a psychiatrist.

The Court: It is for them to obey the order of the Court, and not say what the Court should do.

Mr. Lanham: There is no disposition on their part or our part not to obey the orders of the Court. They say and we think a psychiatrist would be better qualified.

The Court: The local doctors deal in both physical and mental diseases. Mr. Lanham: We feel that it is our duty as members of the bar, and as citizens of the state of South Carolina, in a case like this, which we feel is a mental case and for which something should be done. We don't feel that they are as well qualified to give a competent opinion as a psychiatrist would be. We feel that he should have the benefit of every doubt. We have been appointed to protect his rights; and we feel that only a psychiatrist could give him this greatest benefit.

The Court: You gentlemen were appointed by the Court; and the Court appreciates your very zealous work, and the Court commends you for your evident zeal—it is manifest. The Court, yesterday, offered you full power and authority to order and direct an examination of this defendant with respect to his mental status. It is not for the doctors to suggest to this Court whether they should examine him or not, or whether someone else should do it. The Court won't ask them any questions; and it will attend to them if they refuse to obey the order. It is their duty as professional men to accept the Court's oral order; and, if they don't accept it, the Court will, upon your request, give you a written order.

The defense team's request to postpone was rejected by Judge Mann and the trial began on Thursday as slated.

Following are excerpts of Dolly Jones' direct testimony and cross-examination during the first of the two trials.

Solicitor Watt Cross-Examines the Witness:

> Q. State whether or not he cared about wanting things.
>
> A. e seemed not to care; did not seem to have knowledge enough to care about nothing.
>
> Q. You never did know of him to bring in other piles of money, did you?

A. No, sir.

Re-Cross-Examination by Watt:

Q. Did you ever pick cotton for Mr. Hughes?

A. Yes, sir.

Q. Did he ever go with you, there?

A. I took him along; he has picked cotton with me on Mr. Hughes' place.

Excerpts from the transcript of Lanham's direct examination of Jesse Jones:

Q. Do you know what my name is?

A. Mr. Sam Henry.

Q. Who is the woman that went on the stand here a while ago?

A. I don't know, sir.

Q. That woman said she was your grandmother— is your father living? Have you got a daddy?

A. I have not got nara one.

Q. Have you got a mother?

A. Have not got nara one.

Q. Where do you live?

A. I stay in town, here.

Q. Who do you stay with?

A. I don't know the folks' name.

Q. How long have you been staying there?

A. Been staying there about two (2) months.

Q. Where did you sleep the last time?

A. I stayed in town with some people.

Q. Did you see any bars before the windows?

A. I don't know.

Q. Have you been in jail?

A. I don't know.

Q. You didn't stay in jail last night?

A. Not that I know of.

Q. Do you know Mr. Henry, that man over there?

A. No, sir; do not know him.

Q. Did you know him by the name of Roland Thompson?

A. No, sir; I sure did not.

Q. Did you have a talk with him about going into Mr. Hughes house? Was there another boy with you or not?

A. I can't remember going down there.

Q. Did you tell the officer, Mr. Taylor, that there was another fellow with you when you went down there, that put a spell on you?

A. Yes, sir.

Q. Who was it that put a spell on you?

A. He told me his name was Robert Thompson.

Q. Did he put a spell on you?

A. Yes, sir; he put a spell on me.

Q. What kind of a spell did he put on you?

A. Some kind of funny feeling up in the top of the head—up in here.

Q. What did it feel like?

A. Felt like a snake or something.

Q. What sort of snakes?

A. Large ones; snakes in my bosom too.

Q. How far did they go?

A. Up along here; feel one up there now.

Q. Is that a large one?

A. Pretty good size.

Q. What you say is the trouble with your head?

A. Feel like a lizard going across the side.

Q. Over your eye where you keep putting your hand?

A. Yes, sir.

Q. How came that lizard up there?

A. That boy put a spell on me.

Q. When did this boy put a spell on you?

A. About a week or two.

Q. What did he say to you?

A. He say: "I put a spell on you."

Q. Did he tell you to do anything?

A. He told me to help him go out there and git some money.

Q. Did you go with him?

A. Went with him.

Q. Did you tell the officers you went with him?

A. Yes, sir; but I did not want to go—I couldn't help myself.

Q. Why couldn't you help yourself?

A. He put a spell on me.

Q. Do you hear any voices?

A. Yes, sir.

Q. Did you ever hear any "hants" or spooks?

A. I heard one last night.

Q. Did it make any noise?

A. Curious kind of noise; sort of howling at me.

Q. Did it say anything or just howl or holler at you?

A. Just hollered.

Q. Were you in bed or where?

A. I was in bed, I think.

Q. Do you know what your daddy's name was?

A. I sure don't.

Q. Do you know who your mother was?

A. I don't know.

Q. Do you know who your grandmother is?

A. No, sir; I don't.

Q. You say this boy made you go into that house, did you go in first?

A. He went in first.

Q. How did he go in?

A. Went in the window.

Q. What did he do?

A. He made the first lick.

Q. What did you do?

A. I did not do nothing.

Q. Did you see a shotgun?

A. No, sir.

Q. You did not see that shotgun that's standing up there in the corner now?

A. No, sir; I did not have my hand on it.

Q. How did you get in that window?

A. He went in, first; and I went in behind.

Q. Was the window locked?

A. No, sir.

Q. Did you turn on any light?

A. I did not.

Q. Did you put Mr. Hughes' head on any pillow?

A. No, sir.

Q. How did it get there?

A. I reckon the other boy put it on it.

Q. Did this other fellow put any spell on Mr. Hughes?

A. I don't know whether he did or not; he put one on me.

Q. Where were you when he put the spell on you?

A. Coming along the road from uptown.

Q. How did he do it?

A. Rubbed his hand across there; rubbed his hand across my head there.

Q. What did he say?

A. I am going to put a spell on you.

Q. Have you ever been in jail?

A. Never have.

Q. Where did you spend the night, past night?

A. I can't remember the place's name.

Jones' direct testimony remained confused throughout his examination. The solicitor's most powerful physical evidence, though, was the blood-soaked clothing that had been dropped along the railroad tracks. The jury found Jones guilty, and Judge Mann sentenced him to die by electrocution on June 12, 1942.

Jones' lawyers immediately appealed the sentence, which was subsequently overturned by the South Carolina Supreme Court on the grounds of insufficient mental evaluation. Jones was sent to Columbia, where he was examined by psychiatrists from the state hospital. He was held in a maximum security cell at the main penitentiary. Even though the examining physicians determined that Jones had, at most, the mental capacity of a six-year-old, they considered his mind to be normal for a child of that age, and they reported that he quite possibly knew the difference between right and wrong. The examiners, however, were not firm in their opinion that he fully understood the severity of his actions.

Jones came back to Spartanburg for his second trial, which began on January 8, 1943. The trial, again, took just one day. The jury began deliberations at around seven o'clock that evening. They reached a verdict in less than three hours, and for the second time in less than a year since the Hughes/Petrie murders, Jones stood guilty of murder without a recommendation for mercy. Thus, Judge G. Dewey Oxner of Greenville was left with no option but to impose the maximum sentence. The judge did not immediately pronounce the sentence but stated that he would fix the date of execution the next morning.

When court reconvened, the date of execution was set for the morning of February 19, 1943. Before passing sentence, Judge Oxner praised the work of defense counselors Poliakoff, Lanham, and Frank Bostic, who had replaced Palsay. The judge complimented them for their excellent preparation and diligent defense. The lawyers once again appealed Jones' death sentence, and the date of execution was postponed. However, the appeal was hastily denied and on April 2, 1943, Jones took his seat to "sizzle in the electric chair."

The Spartanburg Herald covered the second trial and sentencing in their editions of January 3, 8, and 9, 1943. The *Herald* also described the execution in their morning edition of April 3,

1943. The *Columbia Record* reported the execution and described the early morning events in the death house in their afternoon edition of April 2, 1943.

The Day of Execution

MY FATHER AND CHAPLAIN E. A. "Lester" Davis visited the death house frequently, sometimes twice daily, during the days leading up to the execution of Jesse Jones, and they both spent several hours with him on the Friday morning before he was put to death.

My father, while convinced that Jones was indeed guilty, was deeply troubled over the execution of one with such obvious mental deficiencies, and Davis was equally troubled.

The Spartanburg Herald reported:

> The prison Chaplain, the Rev. Mr. Kelly, said he visited the Negro yesterday afternoon and again this morning, a short time before he was led into the chamber housing the electric chair.
>
> He appeared very calm, Mr. Kelly said. "He asked us to pray for him and he prayed once himself this morning, just before we left him. He said he felt he had been forgiven for his sins. A minute or two later, though, he was acting as if he didn't realize what was going to happen to him."
>
> Jones was led into the death house by two guards, his right trouser leg rolled above the knee and his head clean shaven. He looked around the room and appeared to smile slightly as he was seated in the chair.

Guards buckled him into the chair, and Capt. C.A. Sullivan, who presides at all executions at the penitentiary, stepped back two paces and asked him, "Jesse, do you have any statement?" The Negro stared at him, apparently not comprehending the question, and the captain asked again, "Do you have anything you want to say?" "Say about which?" the condemned man asked.

"Do you want to say anything?" the guard official asked for a third time.

"What do you mean?" the Negro said.

Dr. M. W. Cheatham, prison doctor, interposed at this point: "He means do you have any statement to make about what you have done?"

"What I done?" the prisoner said, still apparently not comprehending what the officials were asking.

A guard approached with the death mask, and for the first time the Negro seemed to realize how near he was to death's door.

Straining at the leather straps which held him in the chair, he exclaimed in a loud voice, "You've got the wrong one! You don't want to electrocute me!"

Ignoring his protests, guards began strapping the face mask into place.

"You got the wrong one," Jones repeated. "It wasn't me; you got me in the wrong place!"

49

Further protests were muffled as the mask was placed into position, but Jones continued struggling to the full extent of the leather straps. Captain Sullivan warned away one guard who still stood within arm's reach of the chair.

"Stand back," he said.

Captain Sullivan later stated that "had Jones broken free he might have made contact with the guard who could have been killed or badly injured by such contact."

Switch Is Thrown

As the last guard stepped away from the chair, Mr. Cannon threw the switch for the first of three applications of the deadly current. The Negro was raised several inches out of the chair, then settled back into position as the current was released.

Great blisters began forming just below his right knee, where the electrode had been placed. Smoke drifted up around the metal headpiece, and a faint odor of burned human flesh could be smelled. A second charge was administered, and this time, blisters began swelling on his forehead, immediately under the headpiece. The blisters on the leg grew larger, and seemingly threatened to burst.

As the current left his body, Dr. Cheatham advanced for his final examination. He asked that an electric suction fan in the wall above the chair be

stopped and quiet filled the small, crowded room
while the doctor made his examination.

The newspaper also stated that Jones was the 175th person to
be electrocuted by electrician and executioner, Sam Cannon, and
that my father and Davis were accompanied by the Reverend J.
G. Wells, district superintendent for the Church of the Nazarene
in South Carolina, as well as the Reverend L. N. Coggins of
Spartanburg.

The *Herald* report stated that a number of people, including
some police officers, came down from Spartanburg to witness
the execution.

When he understood that his death was imminent, Jesse Jones
had been terrified, and his fear tormented my father, but so, too,
did the terror that Jones had inflicted on his elderly victims as he
swung his ax. Dad wondered: Did the victims have time to scream
for mercy, to plead for their lives as Jones had? In my mind, there
is another irony in this case: Even though Jones was guilty, his
mental deficiency would have spared him the electric chair during
the latter decades of the twentieth century.

Chapter 5
Johnny Sims and Sylvester McKinney

Two young black men, Johnny Sims, seventeen, and Sylvester McKinney, twenty-one, went to their deaths in South Carolina's electric chair on July 16, 1943, for the murder of Walter Cox, a prominent farmer and merchant. Cox was robbed and slain inside his general store in the upstate community of Switzer on the morning of December 23, 1942.

The young men wanted to purchase Christmas presents for friends and family, and they elected to commit the murder of an innocent and hard-working store owner to obtain the cash.

A bread truck driver, who stopped at the store to make a delivery, discovered Cox's body at around 7 a.m., just minutes after the murder. The deliveryman found the blood-soaked body lying on the floor near a basket of apples. Cox's skull had been bashed in.

Spartanburg County law enforcement officials began an immediate investigation but found few clues. However, due to a recent disagreement between Cox and a first cousin in a dispute over a bale of cotton, the cousin became the prime suspect. He was arrested and detained for questioning following an inquest on January 21, 1943. The cousin remained in jail for five weeks, until the last day of February, when Sims and McKinney were apprehended.

The *Spartanburg Herald* reported the youths' arrest on March 2, 1943.

The sub headline and excerpts from the article read:

Further Inquest in Cox Slaying Held Improbable

Early Suspect Absolved after Arrest of Two Negroes

A further inquest into the axe slaying of Walter Cox, Switzer merchant, on the morning of 23 December is improbable, Sheriff Sam M. Henry said yesterday afternoon following the arrest of two negroes who, the sheriff said, had confessed to the crime.

The negroes listed as Johnny Sims, 17, and Sylvester McKinney, 21, both of Woodruff, were arrested yesterday morning in the Woodruff community where they both lived, and were brought to the county jail. Several hours later Sheriff Henry stated they had admitted the slaying.

The mystery surrounding the slaying was cleared for the first time last Saturday, Sheriff Henry said.

"One negro told another negro and that negro told another negro and the thing was out," the sheriff stated.

Before being brought to Spartanburg, McKinney showed the officers the place in the woods two miles from Woodruff where a box containing papers taken from Cox on the morning of the slaying were hidden. The box, buried under a creek bank, was turned over to the sheriff.

Also turned over to the sheriff was an axe which he identified as that used in the killing.

According to several newspaper reports, approximately forty dollars in currency and the metal box filled with papers and a small amount of money in pennies were also taken in the robbery. The two would reveal that one of them took twenty dollars of the larger denomination currency and the other received nineteen dollars as his share. The pennies were then used to make the amounts equal for both partners, with the totals amounting to a little more than twenty dollars each.

Cox opened the store just moments before he was murdered, and he had started to build a fire to ward off the morning chill when Sims and McKinney entered.

The murderers were actually en route to another rural store several miles away with plans to rob and kill the physically handicapped owner, with whom they were acquainted. But while passing the Cox establishment in the early morning darkness, they changed their plan and decided to wait for Cox to open his store.

During pre-trial questioning, as well as in their confessions to my father and Chaplain Lester Davis, Sims and McKinney said that, when they walked into the store, Cox, who knew them, asked what they were planning to do with the ax and that he seemed suspicious. They told him that someone had hired them to kill a hog. Sims asked for half a dozen apples, and as the merchant began to count the apples from a large basket into their bag, one of the men swung the ax and hit him on the side of his face. The blow shattered his jaw, and he collapsed to the floor. As he attempted to stand up, the murderer brought the ax down on the back of his head, crushing his skull.

During questioning, neither Sims nor McKinney admitted swinging the ax, which had been stolen from a neighbor's woodpile. Each man accused the other.

They were both convicted and electrocuted a bit less than seven months after Cox's slaying. Despite the brutality of their crime, my father felt that, had they been reached in time, the young killers could have become law-abiding citizens. Neither Sims nor McKinney seemed vicious to my father, but it was obvious, even to him, that human life was virtually worthless to these two men.

Final Days in the Death House

MY FATHER VISITED THE condemned pair daily during the two weeks they were held in the death house. Their cheerful attitudes amazed him, and he believed their professions of faith in Jesus as their Savior. Even though Sims was illiterate, he was quite intelligent, and he often asked Dad to read certain scriptures for him. McKinney, however, was literate and recited passages from the Bible for himself and his accomplice in the adjacent cell.

Sims and McKinney were among the few condemned prisoners who accepted Dad's offer to stay with them on their last night in the death house. They seemed happy to have my father and Chaplain Davis sitting close by as their final hours ticked away.

The Columbia and Spartanburg newspapers covered the executions and each wrote accounts. The following excerpts are from *The Spartanburg Herald* report published on the morning of July 17, 1943:

> Two young Spartanburg negroes met death this morning in the electric chair of the state penitentiary, admitting with their last moments of life guilt of the murder of Walter Cox, elderly Switzer merchant, and expressing readiness to atone for the crimes with their own lives.

Sylvester McKinney, 21, and Johnny Sims, 18, both of the Woodruff area, were the two negroes executed today.

Both youths appeared calm and resigned to their fate, and both expressed confidence that God had forgiven them for their crime.

Each of the condemned youths entered the crowded death cell singing, McKinney in a clean tenor voice; Sims in lower, more subdued tones.

McKinney Dies Singing

McKinney died first at 7:02 a.m., three minutes and 41 seconds after the switch was thrown, interrupting a spiritual he was singing softly.

Sims followed him to the chair by six minutes and was pronounced dead three minutes and 30 seconds after the current was applied.

About 40 people, half of whom were from Spartanburg, Woodruff and Switzer, filled the little death chamber. Several kin people and friends of the murdered man were among the witnesses. Five women were included in the group.

Spent Quiet Night

Prison chaplains said the two youths spent their last night in this life quietly, frequently joining each other in songs. Sims, an illiterate, listened attentively on several occasions while McKinney read passages from a well-thumbed Bible.

Chaplain C. M. Kelly said McKinney told him last night, "I'm ready to go; I'm not afraid. I'm just as nervous now as I'll ever be, I'm ready to go" and he carried out that promise. He walked calmly into the death chamber singing a spiritual in which the principal refrain was "I'm on My Way to Heaven." He sat down in the chair, leaned his head back and closed his eyes while being buckled into the chair.

On My Way

"I'm on my way to meet my father and mother," he remarked while leaning his head back.

"Sylvester, do you have anything to say?" Assistant Capt. C. A. Sullivan inquired.

The negro opened his eyes and for the first time looked around the room.

"Yessir," he replied, speaking without a trace of nervousness. "I want to say that I'm sorry for what I done. I killed the man. We got $40 from the man. Johnny asked him for some apples and I hit him when he leaned over. That's about all I've got to say."

Chaplain Kelly, as is his custom, leaned forward. "Sylvester, are you saved?"

"Yessir," was the prompt reply, "I'm saved."

Sylvester began to sing again as the mask was being placed over his face. With the mask in place and everyone clear of the chair, Executioner Sam Cannon threw the switch and sent some 2300 volts of electricity surging through his body. Chaplain Kelly told that the body began to burn and that an acrid odor filled the little chamber of death. And that smoke rose from where the cap was fitted over the forehead and from the electrode on the leg.

Conclusion

As Sims sat in the electric chair, he admitted his guilt but denied swinging the ax. His comments were barely audible through his face mask.

With the attending guards standing back, Sullivan tapped his cane on the concrete floor, the signal for the executioner to throw the switch. Electrician Sam Cannon then engaged the switch for the second time that day.

Chapter 6
The Sad Saga of Sammie Osborne

My father described the execution of Sammie Osborne as one of the more distressing events in the criminal history of the state of South Carolina. Dad felt that two human lives were lost needlessly because two strong-willed personalities came together and clashed. Osborne was a seventeen-year-old black youth from the small town of Elco, in Barnwell County. He shot and killed his landlord and employer, W. P. Walker, on the morning of August 17, 1941.

Walker was a respected member of the community who owned a large tract of land that he farmed. Osborne worked for him as field hand. The work was hard, and young Osborne was not always as diligent in his responsibilities as Walker felt that he should be. Thus, conflict was inevitable between the strong-willed Osborne and his equally resolute employer.

Osborne lived alone in one of the shanties on the farm property, as did other laborers who worked there. Osborne testified that bad blood existed between his boss and him, and on successive Saturday mornings prior to the shooting, he said, he and Walker were involved in several confrontations. Nonetheless, even with his life at stake and dependent on his testimony, Osborne seemed evasive and less than forthright in his re-telling of the events of that fateful Saturday, the morning when he and his employer came together in a deadly confrontation. Obviously, the landowner used very poor judgment when he instigated their final encounter, a face-off that would cost both men their lives.

In his court testimony, Osborne stated that on the Saturday morning prior to the shooting, as he lay sick in bed, Walker had broken through the latched door to his shanty and had confronted him with a gun in one hand and a stick in the other. He alleged that Walker had asked if he was going to work that day and that he had responded, "Yes, sir, as soon as I get some breakfast." He stated that Walker answered, "No, you ain't, you going now." He stated that the landowner then forced him out of bed and drove him to the "tator field." Osborne stated that, as they approached the potato field at the edge of Walker's yard, and while they were still in the car Walker uttered a "high oath" and stated, "If you ain't working, I will kill you."

Osborne also testified that, on the Saturday morning preceding the potato field incident; he had gone into town and borrowed ten dollars from the local bank. He stated that Walker saw him in town and that he somehow learned of Osborne borrowing the money. He testified his employer was quite angry over the borrowed cash and because he was in town and not in the fields working. He accused Walker of trying to take the money from him after he had gotten into the car at the farmer's insistence, and, according to Osborne, Walker beat him all the way home.

Once back on the farm, Osborne said, he went into the field and pulled three stalks of fodder. However, Walker returned to the site in his T-Model Ford and allegedly struck Osborne prior to pulling out his pistol and snapping it in Osborne's face. Osborne stated, "I broke and ran and I could hear the weapon snap three more times behind me." Apparently, the gun was not loaded.

On the day of the murder, the evidence showed, Walker was shot while standing over a bed in which Osborne and a friend were lying. Walker owned the shanty, which was occupied by Osborne's friend and the friend's mother.

Osborne was at the friend's house because he, his friend and another young man had gone into nearby Blackville the previous evening and had partied until the wee hours of the morning. Osborne testified that he and his friend had gone to sleep on opposite sides of the bed, within easy reach of two shotguns propped up against the wall. Osborne claimed that he intended to quit his job so, before leaving for Blackville; he had taken his gun, his clothing, and other possessions to the home of the friend.

He awoke when someone began to beat him, he said, and he saw Walker standing beside the bed wielding a stick. There is no way to know for sure what happened in the melee that followed. Osborne's memory failed him at times when he tried to recount the events. But it is a fact that the altercation ended with Walker lying dead on the shanty floor.

Osborne was tried, convicted and sentenced to death approximately one month following the slaying, during the September term of the Barnwell County General Sessions Court. Defense attorneys appealed to the South Carolina Supreme Court, which ordered a new trial. He was retried and, once again, he was convicted and sentenced to death.

His lawyers appealed again at the state level and ultimately to the United States Supreme Court, which refused to hear the case. Osborne was eighteen years old when he received a new execution date: June 4, 1943. The case drew widespread publicity, and the NAACP hired a well-known criminal lawyer, John Stansfield, to represent him.

Stansfield waged a diligent appeals campaign for Osborne and won a stay of execution that kept him alive until November, when his death date was set for the nineteenth. Stansfield had the reputation of being one of the best defense attorneys in South Carolina, and he fought hard to save Osborne, but he could persuade neither the governor nor the courts to intervene.

My father knew that Osborne was guilty of shooting his employer. Indeed, Osborne himself never denied that. However, Dad thought Walker had provoked Osborne and that Osborne had acted in self-defense. He believed that the death sentence was unjust. In an attempt to save Osborne from the chair, Dad asked his friend, Fitzhugh Smith, to help the young man, if he could. Smith was a prominent businessman in Columbia and a member of a state board with involvement at the prisons.

Smith agreed to visit Osborne on the evening of November 16, three days before the execution. I and a World War II soldier stationed at Fort Jackson, Major G. Gatlin, went with Smith and my father to the death house. I was twelve years old.

Smith talked to Osborne for approximately a half hour and seemed ready to take his cause to the governor. However, the then-twelve-year-old author was astounded to hear a defiant Sammie Osborne tell his would-be benefactor that: "I would rather die in the chair on Friday morning than to spend another day in this hell-hole of a prison." Osborne felt he had been wrongly sentenced and he would rather die than to spend years of his life behind the bleak gray walls at the penitentiary.

My father explained that he might one day be released on parole, but Osborne was having none of it. He preferred death over even another day of incarceration, he said. Smith explained that he could only recommend that the governor commute the sentence to life, but Smith said if Osborne indeed preferred death, he would refrain from approaching the governor. Osborne thanked him for his concern, and our group of four departed the death house where Osborne would die in less than seventy-two hours.

On Wednesday, November 17, with less than forty-eight hours to go, the Pardons and Parole Board convened to hear arguments from defense attorney Stansfield. My father and several clergy friends, including Nazarene Evangelist Paul Stewart, attended the special session. They agreed that Stansfield was eloquent and passionate in his pleas for Osborne's life, but the panel was unmoved.

Governor Olin D. Johnston went to visit Osborne that evening. There is no way to know what was said, but there is little doubt the governor was searching for and would have welcomed a reason to spare Sammie Osborne's life. Johnston was leaving no stone unturned.

Reasonable speculation would indicate that Osborne rejected the governor's probable offer to intervene in much the same manner he had rebuffed Smith's willingness to try and help. Nonetheless, when the governor took his leave from the death house, the fate of Sammie Osborne was sealed with his departure.

My father, Gatlin, and I visited Osborne again on the night before his execution. I will never forget that night. Osborne stood in his cell with a towel covering his bald head to ward off the chill.

Dad offered to return to the death house at around midnight to keep Osborne company, and Osborne thanked him, but, he said, he planned to get a good night's sleep.

The execution was scheduled for seven o'clock, but at the request of Dr. M. Whitfield Cheatham, the attending physician at all executions, the time for Osborne to take his seat in the chair was postponed by thirty minutes. The following excerpts are from the *Columbia Record* of November 19, 1943:

> Sammie Osborne, 20-year-old Negro, twice convicted of the killing of W. P. Walker, prosperous Barnwell county landowner, died in the electric chair at the state penitentiary at 7:33 a. m. today with a denial of guilt still on his lips.

> Walker was killed on August 17, 1941 when he entered a house in which Osborne was staying. Osborne contended at his trial that he acted only in self-defense.

> Asked by a prison official if he had anything to say, Osborne who had been smiling and nodding

to a few acquaintances replied, "I'm not guilty of killing Mr. Walker. I don't know anything about it. I believe that I could have cleared myself if I had more time but I begged the governor to give me more time and to pardon me but he wouldn't do it."

The news article also said that over a score of spectators were present to witness the execution and that among them were Walker's brother and a cousin.

Chapter 7
Sammy Joe "Frank" Timmons

S ammy Joe "Frank" Timmons was executed on the morning of Friday, May 12, 1944. This young black man had attended school through the fourth grade, when he was taken out of class to work in the fields. He was born in the crossroads community of Evergreen, which is in the northeastern part of South Carolina, near the small city of Florence. Timmons was not even sure of his age but thought himself to be around twenty.

The *Columbia Record*'s Mark Warren wrote a column about the case that was published on May 10, 1944. Warren interviewed Timmons, who spoke with the vocabulary and speech patterns common to rural Carolina in that era. When Warren asked Timmons his age, he responded, "I don't know my age, but thinks I'm most twenty." When asked about his family, he said that he was married but added, "My wife ... done quit me." Timmons claimed to have a young daughter whose age he didn't know, but he guessed she was "most three."

He confirmed that for the past three years he had worked on a farm in Horry County that was only a few miles out of Loris. It was during that time he met the woman who would become his wife and the mother of his child.

In most cases, condemned inmates had a lawyer, a civil rights organization, or other interested parties fighting to save them.

However, no last minute appeals were made on Timmons' behalf, and Governor Olin D. Johnston saw no reason to intervene.

World War II raged during the 1940s, and Timmons lied about his age when he tried to join the Army. He listed his age as eighteen but thought that he was only seventeen. Timmons never told why he was rejected for induction, but he seemed sincere about wanting to serve his country. If so, fate was not kind to Frank Timmons.

Timmons, by his own admission, was responsible for his situation. He had gone to the home of a white woman, he said, with the intent to steal a jacket belonging to her husband, and the terrified woman found him inside her house. However, Timmons is quoted as saying, "I went in and gets the jacket but I never lays no hand on her. She just screamed, and when I went by she stuck me with an ice pick."

My father stated that Timmons steadfastly denied any objective beyond the theft of the jacket, and in the moments before he was taken from his cell to be executed, he plaintively denied any intent to attack the woman.

Though Dad was not totally convinced by Timmons' story, he was prone to believe that theft was his only motive. It is possible that as he attempted to avoid the ice pick, he grabbed the woman by the arm, as Timmons said. For that instant of physical contact he was charged with attempted criminal assault, a charge that meant an almost certain death sentence for any black man convicted of that offense against a white woman during the 1940s.

One can understand the terror of the victim upon discovering an unknown man in her home. She was more than justified in her attempt to stab him to death, and had she succeeded, she would have faced no criminal charges. The innocent woman was as much the victim as was Timmons when he took his seat in the chair. The victimization process began when Timmons, by his own admission, deliberately violated her home to steal her husband's jacket.

Timmons fled the scene of the crime and hid in the woods near Loris, where a posse of a hundred and fifty men found him. They chased him through the woods, and a police officer shot at him twice. A state highway patrolman fired a third shot in his direction before he was apprehended. He was hurriedly tried and convicted, and his life of poverty was exchanged for something even worse, a jail cell and death in the electric chair.

Timmons claimed to have been surprised when he was charged for attempted criminal assault. He said that he had never been to Conway, the county seat, prior to going there for his first trial. He was advised that it would be better for him to plead guilty to the charges, but he did not know until much later what that meant, he said.

Timmons told a reporter that he was worried about being electrocuted, but when the time came, he walked quietly from his cell and took his seat in the chair.

Some fifty witnesses were present for the execution, including James W. Cox, then chief of police in the Columbia suburb of Cayce. Cox was the Loris police officer who fired shots at the fleeing Timmons when he was arrested.

Timmons was twice asked if he had anything to say. Both times, he just shook his head in the negative. His final words had been addressed to my father and Chaplin E. A. "Lester" Davis only minutes earlier. He told them that he was ready and prepared to meet his maker.

Executioner Sam Cannon threw the switch and some twenty-three hundred volts of electrical current surged into Timmons' body. Frank did not die easily. It took a second series of jolts and more than five minutes for him to be pronounced dead.

His body was claimed by his parents and sent back to his boyhood home near the city of Florence for burial.

Chapter 8
George Stinney Jr. and Bruce Hamilton

T he cases of these youths had little in common except that both young black men took their seats in the electric chair on Friday, June 16, 1944. George Junius Stinney Jr., who was only fourteen years of age when he murdered two young white girls on March 24 of that same year, was the first to die. The fourteen-year-old Stinney was then and remains the youngest person ever to be electrocuted by the State of South Carolina. In fact, he is believed to be the most youthful person ever put to death in that state and perhaps the United States under the provisions of capital punishment. The small girls Stinney was accused of killing were Betty June Binnicker, eleven, and Mary Emma Thames, who was only eight when she was slain.

The deadly rampage for which Stinney was put to death happened during a springtime afternoon in the small town of Alcolu, in Clarendon County. The girls had gone out to search for the wild honeysuckle vines from which the fragrance was filling the air when they came upon young George J. Stinney Jr. The happy duo inquired if Stinney knew where to find the vines and he responded that he did. He suggested that they follow him and he would take them to the honeysuckle. For whatever their reasons, the girls declined his offer to guide and they went their separate ways.

The afternoon wore on, and everyone became anxious when the girls did not return home for supper. And their concern turned to panic when the pair did not return to the safety of their homes at sundown. Their residences were less than a hundred feet apart, and the terrified parents stayed in fearful contact as the day faded into twilight. Police were notified, and the call for a search party spread throughout the community. Volunteers responded and the quest to find the missing girls began during the early evening.

Children in Alcolu simply did not go missing in 1944. And, as word of the vanished pair spread into nearby areas, additional volunteers joined the search that lasted throughout the night. By daybreak, the ranks of rescuers had swollen to more than one hundred individuals who were determined to find the missing children. Then, shortly after sunup on March 25, 1944, two of the searchers were probing the undergrowth near some railroad tracks when they found the lifeless bodies.

The pair of searchers, Donald Padgett and Francis Batson, was prying into the bushes along a ditch near the Alderman Lumber Company when they made the gruesome discovery. The small corpses of Betty June Binnicker and Mary Emma Thames were lying partly submerged in the stagnant waters of the trench from which a light mist was rising. Word of finding the lifeless remains was circulated to the helpers and the search was finished. The little girls were brutally murdered, and the killer had attempted to conceal the crime by placing the bodies in the drainage ditch.

George Stinney Jr. was arrested only hours after the bodies were discovered. And during the questioning that began immediately, he told the interrogators that he had twice come upon the girls the previous afternoon. And that when he saw them the second time, they had found the honeysuckle vines and they were then busy gathering the flowers.

Murders Announced and Stinney Arrested

ON MARCH 25, 1944, authorities in Alcolu released a brief account of the crime and the arrest of George Stinney. The Associated Press news bulletin was picked up and carried on the front page of the *Columbia Record* under the sub-headline:

> Two Alcolu Children Are Found Slain
>
> Coroner C. M. Thigpen said today two little girls who left their homes together to pick flowers yesterday afternoon were found dead in a ditch near the Alderman Mills in Clarendon County about dawn this morning.
>
> The coroner said the girls, one six [sic] years of age and the other nine [sic] years, apparently had been beaten to death.
>
> The children were found by Donald Padgett and Francis Batson, members of a searching party that was organized when the little girls failed to return to their homes at nightfall, Thigpen said.
>
> Clarendon County Sheriff H. S. Newman said this afternoon that George Junius, 14, told officers he beat to death two little Alcolu girls. Newman said Junius led police to a hidden piece of iron which the youth told officers was the death weapon.

Only George Stinney ever knew exactly what happened following his encounters with the girls. And no one will ever know what instigated young Stinney to commit the murders. However, those chance meetings between the girls and the fourteen-year-old resulted in the premature deaths of all three. At the time of his execution, Stinney was four and a half months shy of his fifteenth birthday.

A moderate amount of news coverage was given to the pending execution, and Stinney never denied the murders. In fact, on June 13, 1944, only three days preceding the Stinney/Hamilton execution, the *Columbia Record* reported:

> In the presence of witnesses at the death house at the state penitentiary, George Junius Stinney Jr., 14, convicted murderer, today made a full confession that he bludgeoned to death two little girls, one 8 and the other 11, on 24 March at Alcolu.
>
> "Which one did you kill first?" asked Captain B. Frank Wilkes, captain-of-the-guard at the prison.
>
> "The smaller girl," Stinney replied. "Then I hit the big one."
>
> "What did you hit them with?"
>
> "A piece of iron," Stinney said.
>
> He related that he first met the pair and they asked him if he knew where the honeysuckle was growing. He said he told them he did and would show them. How He Did It
>
> After they left, he related that he picked up an iron spike from the railroad and accosted them again. He killed the younger girl, and then her companion, he said.
>
> Stinney was reluctant to speak on the subject at first and then said he "couldn't remember." Once on the topic of how the crime occurred, he readily

related beating both girls with the spike. Their bodies were found in a ditch the following day.

Stinney said he was born at Pinewood, Sumter County, on October 24, 1929. He said he was finishing the seventh grade at the time he was arrested, March 25.

Stinney was reading his Bible when visited in the death house and resumed reading it as his callers prepared to depart. He appeared nervous when the subject of death was mentioned.

Nothing in our search of microfilmed newspaper reports, letters to Governor Olin Johnston, court records, and other files revealed how police connected George Stinney Jr. to the murders. Even so, the authorities somehow linked Stinney to the dead girls, and he repeatedly admitted the slayings to my father and other ministers. He not only confessed he led the arresting officers to the fourteen-inch railroad spike he used to smash the skulls of the two little girls.

Stinney was said to have told police that he killed the smaller child first because his intent was to rape the older one. He was afraid that the younger girl might run and tell he assaulted her friend. According to interrogators, he disclosed that after battering the head of the smaller Mary Emma, he turned his thoughts to forcing himself on the eleven-year-old Betty June. She resisted his advances and, to keep her from talking, he resorted to the use of the heavy iron spike to ensure that she never spoke again.

During questioning, Stinney confessed freely to the killings, but when asked about his intent to violate the older girl, he always claimed not to remember, even until the moments just prior to his execution. It seems to have never been reported publicly but it was rumored that he attempted to rape the lifeless body of the eleven-year-old. That disgusting rumor, if true, was almost certainly the reason for Stinney's selective amnesia. Even though he repeatedly acknowledged the pair of murders, he seemed ashamed to discuss his alleged intent to rape the older child. However, that rumor refused to die.

Letters to Governor Johnston

ONE MENTION OF STINNEY'S attempt to have sex with the lifeless body of the older girl was made by none other than Governor Johnston. The governor revealed this charge in his response to a concerned citizen who had, because of Stinney's age, written a letter protesting the execution. An excerpt from the governor's exchange with the letter writer is as follows:

> I have just talked with the officer making the arrest in this case. It may be interesting for you to know that Stinney killed the smaller girl to rape the larger one. Then he killed the larger girl and raped her dead body. Twenty minutes later he returned to rape her again but her body was too cold. All of this, he admitted himself. ... One other thing, the colored people of Alcolu would have lynched this boy themselves had it not been for the protection of the officer.
>
> Sincerely yours, Olin D. Johnston, Governor

The gentleman to whom the governor's remarks were addressed scribbled a response back to Johnston in the blank space at the bottom of the governor's response to him. It read:

> Dear Mr. Johnston, I did not question the guilt of the boy, nor the horror of his crime! I simply know that the state should not kill a minor. He

deserved worse than death, of course. What he
did and deserved is not the basis for my protest,
but our right to put him to death.

There were many such letters to the governor. Some writers
favored the sentence being imposed immediately while others
were strong in their statements against the execution of the
fourteen-year-old. Stinney was viewed by some as a hapless
victim, a child whose tender age dictated that he be spared the
lethal sentence. Other blatantly racist messages demanded that
the sentence to be imposed without delay.

Following are excerpts from letters and telegrams that were
sent to Johnston in favor of or in protest of the Stinney execution.

A telegram dated June 15, 1944, from man in Cleveland, Ohio:

To execute the fourteen year old Negro child
will be more gruesome and horrible than the
crime he committed. I beseech you not to carry
out execution.

From a letter dated June 13, 1944, from a man in Miami, Florida:

I know of nothing the state could gain by
executing a child. ... I am a native of Florida, my
father is from North Carolina and I certainly do not
love the negroes. I only wish they were all back in
Africa where they came from. However, there is
enough grief in the world without adding to it.

From a letter dated June 10, 1944, from a rabbi in Charleston,
South Carolina:

Like many of our citizens, I feel impelled to
call your attention to the case of George Stinney,
the fourteen year old Negro boy, who has been

sentenced to die on the sixteenth, and ask you to take into consideration his background, environment, education, mentality, etc., that must have had bearing upon his behavior. I make bold to urge it upon you not only for humanitarian reasons, since he is a minor, but with the thought of the ignominy which his execution may bring upon the fair name of our state.

From a letter dated June 12, 1944, from a doctor in Lake City, South Carolina:

As a physician, permit me to say that this class of criminals are [sic] regarded as a "sexual pervert" and no punishment can be imposed upon them that will change their disposition. Therefore, I trust you will not interfere with the sentence of the Court, but let the Negro boy be electrocuted at the date set next Friday, June 16th.

From a letter dated June 14, 1944, from an unknown individual in Florence, South Carolina:

I was shocked and amazed to find the enclosed advertisement in our daily paper. This sends chills through the spine to think what we white people could expect in the way of justice from the negro should he rule. Why mercy for this little rattle snake? Has he shown mercy to his 2 little white victims? He cut them down in the bloom of life. The sooner such as him are removed from our midst the safer we all feel. Let the law take its course and terminate the sinister life of this reptile. In that way you can avoid lynching's [sic].

From a letter dated June 9, 1944, from a man in Mullins, South Carolina:

> I am writing to say that I am by no means in favor of saving this fellow's life. ... It may be that if his life is saved, with many negro boys, it will mean that they may rape and kill white girls without any fear of punishment other than life imprisonment and with the hope of pardon at some future date.

From a second letter by the same man in Charleston, South Carolina, dated June 6, 1944:

> I will not worry you with this matter again, but I am going to appeal to you for this negro child's life once more, Governor, in the name of all Christian justice, and for the sake of our beloved state, because I despise to hear people from the North and outside generally, speak of South Carolinians as if they are living in Mediaeval times.

From a letter dated June 5, 1944, from a woman in Charleston, South Carolina:

> Hard cold facts. The crime was brutal without the shadow of a doubt, but the sentence was more brutal. It would seem to me that a wrong is not righted by another wrong. Has it ever occurred to anyone that this child may be a potential moron, that he may have glandular trouble that would cause anyone, white or black, young or old to do things for which he was not responsible? However, the state is losing sight of the fact that all her children are brothers under the skin, no matter what the color. You, Mr. Governor, have made it

known that you can do nothing about the matter. You, Mr. Governor, are perhaps one of the few that can do something about the matter, as is common knowledge. It is highly incongruous that a group of people would elect a man to have charge over their affairs and give him the power of life and death, where his judgment is questionable.

From a letter dated June 12, 1944, from a man in Greenville, South Carolina:

It gives me great pleasure to note the stand you [have] taken in regards to the execution of George Stinney. I am also glad to note the stand you take in the Negro voting question, which could bring about a serious condition. I hope you will have enough man power at your command to handle the situation. I wish that there was some way to keep so much Negro propaganda out of the newspapers as it don't [sic] serve any useful purpose.

From a 2nd Lieutenant, USMCR, in a letter dated June 12, 1944:

This morning's paper brought to my attention the capital sentence to be given to a 14-year-old Negro boy, George Stinney Jr., of Alcolu, on the 16th of this month. Excepting a case of mental deficiency, it seems rather inconceivable to me that people calling themselves civilized could consent to such a sentence.

From the executive secretary, Southern Negro Youth Congress, Birmingham, Alabama, in a letter dated June 14, 1944:

My dear Gov. Johnston,

The best sons of South Carolina, both white and Negro, are giving their lives on the continent of Europe and in the islands of the Pacific in supreme sacrifices to free the conquered peoples of the world from the German and Japanese tyrannies. All over the world they are fighting and dying to preserve world civilization and the future existence of our Country as a land of the free from the heavy hand of the fasciest [sic] barbarians. Among the crimes of our enemies is recorded the supreme crime of the executioners of little children; as witness Lidice, Polish, and Russian towns. Let history not record that the democratic state of South Carolina by an act of the chief executive set its seal upon a court order directing the execution of a 14 year old child. We urge you to wave [sic] the death penalty in the case of 14 year old George Junius Stinney, Negro lad charged with murder: Vindictive violence against children is surely recognized by you as a part of the Hitler pattern and no matter the provocation has no justification in the eyes of the enlightened citizenry of your State and our Nation. Trusting that this appeal will receive your sympathetic consideration, I am respectfully yours...

From a letter dated June 14, 1944, from a woman in Williamsburg, Virginia:

> I am a southerner, from the deep south, the black belt of Alabama. I played with negroes all my childhood and attended the funeral in the company of my father, in a pine grove near our home, of his slave wet nurse Aunt Mariah. In her latter years, she had been cared for by my father. She lived in a one room cabin near our home and had shared her chickens and sweet potatoes with us children. I believe I understand negroes and I have great respect for the integrity of many of them, and a greater desire to see my race settle amicably the problems that must necessarily arise between it and the negro race. If this fourteen year old boy had been white, he would have been considered a juvenile and treated as such. I am entering my plea for the equality of this and other people of like quality before the law.

In the old south of the early 1900s and during prior centuries, many white mothers engaged the services of lactating Negro women, many times their slave or household servant, to breast feed their infants. Such relationships produced an affectionate bond between white children and their Negro "aunties." The descriptive title "wet nurse" is the letter writer's reference to "Aunt Mariah," who had been a source of affection and sustenance for her own father when he was but a toddler.

Dad Visits the Governor

My father used the open-door status he had received from Governor Johnston to make a plea for mercy during Stinney's final few days. He voiced his concerns and asked the governor to consider a commutation of the sentence to life in prison for the condemned youth. The minister knew from Stinney's own admissions to him and his clergy colleagues that the fourteen-year-old was guilty. However, like many individuals who had written the governor, Dad was troubled by the execution of one so young. The governor listened to my father's concerns and, as was his nature, Johnston was gracious and cordial with his prisons cleric whom he always addressed as "Preacher." However, my father told that the governor ended the visit with the following words: "Preacher, I share your concern over executing one who is only fourteen. And the letters both for and against the execution make my decision extremely difficult. But, despite his tender age, the enormity of the crime for which he is certainly guilty causes executive clemency to be without merit."

During his visit with the governor, my father also appealed for the life of Bruce Hamilton. Hamilton, unlike Stinney who was admitting his guilt, was adamant that he was innocent of the assault with intent to rape conviction for which he was sentenced to death. Hamilton had a new lawyer, John Schofield, who had filed a last minute appeal with the state Supreme Court, and the governor would not consider clemency until the court made its ruling. The appeal was denied, but even then the tenacious Schofield continued his efforts to save the life of his client by personally visiting Governor Johnston.

The Executions

TWO DAYS FOLLOWING MY father's visit with the governor, Stinney made his final confession to the chaplains during the hour before he was escorted into the execution chamber. The youngster was slight of build and in much the same manner as it had been with Sue Logue some seventeen months prior, it was necessary to punch additional holes in the chairs leather bindings before they would fit snugly around his limbs. The hole punching procedure delayed the execution for some agonizing minutes as the fourteen-year-old Stinney sat calmly awaiting his fate.

The Columbia Record reported the executions on June 16, 1944. The article stated, "Young Stinney was such a small boy that it was difficult to adjust the electrode to his right leg. After the first charge of 2400 volts was sent coursing through his body, the death mask slipped from his face and his eyes were open when two additional shots of 1400 and 500 volts followed."

Dad described an even more vivid picture of Stinney's face when the mask slipped. He told of the eyes bulging almost from their sockets and of the tortured facial grimaces that came with each jolt of electrical current.

The news report stated that the fathers of the two girls and a brother of the older girl were present to see Stinney put to death. One father exclaimed "I'm satisfied," as Stinney's body was lifted from the chair. It was further stated that a large number of Clarendon County residents, including Sheriff J. Edward Gamble, were present for the execution which took three minutes and forty-five seconds.

The newspaper write up revealed that witnesses began talking as Stinney entered the execution chamber and that it had been necessary for the superintendent to demand quiet.

My father told that it was common for observers to whisper among themselves when a doomed inmate entered the death chamber and that the reaction to Stinney was not unusual. He affirmed that, several times during his death chamber experiences, it had been necessary for the superintendent to go beyond rapping his cane on the floor and to verbally demand quiet and respect for the somberness of the occasion. However, with the fourteen-year-old youth, the superintendent needed only to rap his cane several times on the concrete floor to restore the dignity of silence as George Stinney made his way to the chair.

The news report related that, when asked, "Do you have anything to say?" Stinney chose to remain silent. The question was asked by the captain of the guard in charge of executions and repeated by Dr. M. Whitfield Cheatham. To both, Stinney simply responded, "No, Sir."

Unreported Events in the Hearse

MY FATHER TOLD THAT Stinney's body was claimed and as the vehicle transporting the deceased neared the city of Sumter, attendants heard what they described as a sigh coming from the back of the hearse. They checked the corpse for any sign of life and were surprised to detect a very faint heartbeat. They called the penitentiary and someone in authority directed them take the body to a physician in Sumter who would be notified of their coming by Dr. Cheatham.

The Sumter physician found the heartbeat had ceased and the grim journey to the burial service at Pinewood was allowed to continue. This incident was never reported publicly and had not my father remained at the prison to attend to some additional duties, he would not have known of the situation in the hearse.

The Sad Lack of Concern for Bruce Hamilton

NOTHING CONNECTS THE CASES of George Stinney to Bruce Hamilton except that both were electrocuted on the morning of June 16, 1944. Each was convicted on unrelated charges in separate jurisdictions and their executions on the same day were nothing more than coincidence. However, manifest in the cases of the two black youths are examples of situations that were present in that era of segregation.

Those flawed standards were evident in both cases but were especially so in the conviction and execution of Bruce Hamilton. Stinney, because of his age, would have escaped execution in the latter years of the twentieth century, even though he was self-admittedly guilty. However, societal conditions of the 1940s were at least partially responsible for the execution of Bruce Hamilton who denied his guilt.

Hamilton was arrested on the charge of assault with intent to ravish, and questioned under the often brutal practices that were common during that era. Poverty stricken and poorly educated, Hamilton was without legal representation when he was questioned.

He had been apprehended some weeks following the brutal assault on a WW-II soldier's wife, and he was returned to Spartanburg for questioning. He told that he had gone to Georgia to visit relatives after quitting his job delivering furniture for a store in Greenville, a job he left just days prior to the assault.

Spartanburg authorities began questioning Hamilton immediately upon his return from Atlanta and after some intense hours of grilling, he confessed. At a hastily called news conference, Hamilton made a public declaration of his guilt. Police authorities were anxious to calm the fears of women throughout the upstate area and they needed the radio and newspaper reporters to put out the news of Hamilton's arrest and subsequent admission of guilt following his interrogation.

The Hamilton Trial

THE SPARTANBURG HERALD REPORTED on April 28, 1944, that Hamilton had confessed to the arresting officers, and that on direct examination, both officers stated that no threats or promises had been made to secure his admission. The officers stated they had advised Hamilton that he did not have to make a statement.

No defense witness, not even Hamilton, was called to testify or to offer rebuttal to the assault charges. The young victim, to her eternal credit, refused to identify Hamilton as the man who attempted to rape her. She had no interest in convicting an innocent man. She testified that she had scratched her assailant's face, bitten his hand, and smashed his head with a rock, but no one was called to confirm or deny that anyone had seen evidence of such injuries when he was arrested.

Nothing found during research indicated in what way Hamilton had been connected to the crime or how the authorities had located him in Atlanta. His only link to the felony seemingly stemmed from his having delivered a load of furniture from a store in Greenville to an address in the apartment complex where the young woman lived in Spartanburg. He made the delivery just days prior to the assault but there was no indication that Hamilton had been in contact with the victim. His only connection to the crime was seemingly involved with him quitting his job and returning to his native Georgia at about the time of the assault.

Hamilton was represented by a pair of court appointed attorneys, Paul Taylor and J. L. Lancaster. But, due to his public confession at the news conference following his return to Spartanburg, his lawyers were reluctant to expose him to cross-examination.

The attorneys argued that, due to the radio and newsprint coverage of his confession, it was impossible for Bruce Hamilton, to receive a fair trial in Spartanburg County. The prosecutor countered that extensive coverage of the arrest and confession was clearly necessary to calm the fears of frightened female citizens throughout the local area.

Despite the methods used to report Hamilton's confession, the judge denied the motion for a change of venue and there was little they could do to avert the guilty verdict and mandatory death sentence.

Judge M. M. Mann, of St. Matthews passed the death sentence following the verdict. However, until the moment the switch was thrown, Hamilton denied his guilt and protested that he was not even in Spartanburg at the time of the attack. Nonetheless, and with there being clear probability that Hamilton was innocent, he received no outcry of public support. Except for his court appointed attorneys, Paul Taylor and J. L. Lancaster, and eventually John Schofield, Hamilton was a forgotten man.

Organizations dedicated to minority grievances were involved in efforts to spare the fourteen-year-old Stinney, even though he frequently admitted his guilt. Those same groups, however, made no effort on behalf of Bruce Hamilton the young man who stood convicted and sentenced to death on the weakest of hypothetical evidence. Hamilton's link to the crime was weak and circumstantial.

Hamilton's trial lawyers were replaced by John M. Schofield, an upcoming defense attorney from Greenville who fought doggedly to save his clients. He used whatever means necessary to satisfy his responsibilities and that trait sometimes caused him to seem biased. However, Schofield cared not that his client was white or black or whether he received payment for his services. He felt strongly that it was his job to defend them, and, defend them he did.

On April 28, 1944, *The Spartanburg Herald* reported that the jury deliberated two hours and twenty-five minutes in the Hamilton case, before bringing out a verdict of guilty without a recommendation for mercy. The article further reported that:

> Solicitor Sam Watt introduced yesterday as the state's first witness in the Hamilton case, the victim of the attack. The young woman, wife of a soldier who at that time was stationed at Camp Croft and has since been sent overseas, told of being grabbed by a Negro with whom she fought and who attempted to assault her. She testified further that the attack was not completed because of her struggling and because of the approach of a car. The prosecuting witness testified that the Negro man grabbed her, placed his hand over her mouth, dragged her over a ditch into the woods in the Duncan Park area, and attempted to criminally attack her. She told of struggling with the Negro, of striking him over the head with a rock, scratching his face and biting his hand. She said however that she was unable to identify her assailant.

In addition, the newspaper reported testimony by detectives concerning Hamilton's confession, but there was still no indication of how he was connected to the assault or what led them to seek him in Atlanta some two months following the attack. The trial lasted less than two full days, but, when finished, Hamilton stood convicted and only weeks away from his appointment with the executioner.

John Schofield Appeals to the Governor

THE DETERMINED YOUNG ATTORNEY, after denial of his appeal to the high court, drove to Columbia on the day before the execution to plead with Governor Johnston to spare the life of Bruce Hamilton. And in response to the appeals by my father and attorney Schofield the governor sent Dr. Baxter Funderburk, chairman of the Pardons and Parole Board, to the death house to talk with Hamilton. However, with only hours remaining to live, the soon-to-be executed youth could reveal nothing to Funderburk that would change the dreaded outcome.

The Morning of the Execution

ON JUNE 16, 1944, the *Columbia Record*'s Mark Warren wrote that Hamilton's final words were, "I am willing to die and someday in heaven I hope to meet the person who has caused me to sit in this chair." The newspaper also reported that just before the switch was thrown, Hamilton muttered, "I ain't done it, I ain't done it."

On June 17, 1944, *The Spartanburg Herald* reported:

> According to State Electrician Sam Cannon, Hamilton's death required four minutes and four seconds. The younger negro's death consumed three minutes and 45 seconds. Cannon, who has officiated at state executions for almost 30 years, said he used a new method of electrocution

on Hamilton. Instead of two heavy shocks of electricity as customarily used, he used a series of short shocks. The new method, he said, is designed to reduce the time of suffering by the condemned person.

Obviously, there is confusion between *The Spartanburg Herald* report on the Stinney/Hamilton executions and other executions handled by electrician Sam Cannon. The *Columbia Record's* Mark Warren always reported that three high voltage shocks were used prior to the body being examined to determine if the person was dead. My father also told that three shocks were administered beforehand. And that sometimes following the physician's examination that even more jolts of electrical current were necessary to bring on death. Based on descriptions of executions by Mark Warren and my father, it seems that Sam Cannon either misspoke or was somehow misquoted by *The Spartanburg Herald*.

AUTHOR'S NOTE: IN 2014, a circuit court judge vacated the murder conviction of George Stinney. The judge did not address Stinney's guilt or innocence, but she ruled that his constitutional rights had been violated.

Chapter 9
Hurley Jones

H urley Jones was a twenty-two-year-old black man, a third-grade dropout and laborer from Greenville who went to his death on Friday, November 3, 1944. His life was taken as punishment for the senseless rape of a seventeen-year-old white girl, just after he had attended a vaudeville show where he had partaken heavily from a whiskey bottle.

My father was out of town for the Jones execution. However, he visited the youth on numerous occasions during the days preceding Jones taking his final walk. Dad's friend and colleague, the Reverend C. F. Wimberly, substituted for him on the morning Hurley Jones was strapped into the unforgiving chair. In addition to Wimberly, Chaplain E. A. Davis, and one of his clergy friends, the Reverend S. M. Hightower, was also present to offer spiritual comfort.

Reporting the execution for the *Columbia Record* on the afternoon of November 3, 1944, reporter Mark Warren, wrote that Jones was visited by a female cousin shortly before his death but she had not stayed to witness the execution. The young relative revealed that Hurley had fully confessed to committing the crime in the presence of his parents. She told that Hurley had lived in Washington, D.C., as well as in the upstate city of Greenville, where he was born. She also affirmed that the body would be claimed and returned to Greenville where a funeral service was scheduled for Sunday afternoon.

Chaplain Davis stated that Jones had also confessed to him during his visit on Thursday, the day before he was executed. Davis revealed that following the confession, Jones had repented of his sins and then requested to be baptized. Permission was granted and Davis did the honors on that Thursday afternoon.

My father stated that several times during his visits that Jones had confessed to the crime and stated that he had accepted Christ as his savior.

Excerpts from the Warren Column:

> Hurley Jones (22) of Greenville died in the electric chair shortly after 7:00 o'clock this morning at the state penitentiary after mumbling a prayer for those present and for himself.
>
> Jones, who confessed several times to the rape of a 17-year-old girl, May 1, at Greenville was apparently frightened at the prospect of death.
>
> Clutching his Bible in his left hand as he was being strapped into the chair, Jones said indistinctly: "I hope to meet each and every one of you in Heaven. May God have mercy."
>
> The state electrician, Sam Cannon, then pulled the switch sending 2300 volts into Jones' body and 4:33 minutes later Dr. M. Whitfield Cheatham, prison physician, pronounced the prisoner dead.
>
> Even after four minutes from the time the current was turned on, Jones' right hand continued to move convulsively.

The report stated that some sixty witnesses, including two white women, were present for the execution of the sad-eyed youth from Greenville. Among the observers were a number of police officers who had participated in the investigation following the sexual assault on the young woman back in May of that same year.

Jones was arrested quickly, and following a brief trial, he was found guilty of assaulting a young white female, a capital offense. On September 7, 1944, immediately following the jury's verdict, Judge E. H. Henderson sentenced Hurley Jones to death in the electric chair and set the date of execution to be on November 3rd.

The sentence was not appealed, and Jones was admitted to the penitentiary in Columbia on October 15. There he would spend the final eighteen days of his life as he awaited his date with the executioner.

Chapter 10
Death by Gas in North Carolina

During the early evening of December 26, 1944, the phone rang in our home and it was the governor's secretary calling. She was relaying the message that Governor Olin D. Johnston wanted my father to journey up to the North Carolina State Penitentiary in Raleigh to witness a trio of gas chamber executions. The executions were scheduled for the morning of December 29, and the governor needed an immediate answer as to whether dad could make the trip.

Johnston was interested in Dad's opinion as to whether the electric chair or the gas chamber was the more humane way to snuff out a human life. He felt that since Dad had been present to witness a number of those put to death in the electric chair, that by having him witness the gas chamber executions in the neighboring state, that my father could offer an informed observation of which method caused the least suffering.

Dad confirmed that he could make the trip, and the governor's staff rushed through the arrangements with their counterparts in North Carolina. My father was met at the train station in Raleigh and taken to a hotel to spend Thursday night. Early on Friday morning, a staff car came and took him to the prison. There he had the opportunity to talk for several hours with the three individuals who were executed that morning as well as with fellow chaplains, guards and prison officials.

All three of the doomed were typically nervous but the young black woman, Bessie Mae Williams, was quite emotional. Dad told that she would intermittently break down and weep as she neared the end of her very brief life. Bessie, a nineteen-year-old and her partner, eighteen-year-old Ralph Thompson, also black, were convicted of the robbery/slaying of a Charlotte taxi driver. Veteran police officers stated publicly that the crime was the most brutal they had ever investigated, and several of those officers were present for the executions.

Another young African-American woman, fourteen-year-old Annie Mae Allison, was similarly involved in the slaying in a dispute over cab fare. And she too had been sentenced to die. However, Governor Broughton, because of her tender age, had commuted her sentence to life. According to the governor, he acted only out of consideration of her age.

Cleve Johnson, twenty-four, was likewise involved in the cabbies slaying. He, though, turned state's evidence and pleaded his charge down to second-degree murder to escape the death penalty. He received a sentence of from twenty-five to thirty years but he would subsequently escape and flee to a location in Ohio. He was soon captured and returned to North Carolina to serve out his years in the North Carolina prison.

In addition to Bessie Williams and Ralph Thompson, another young black man was put to death on that cold morning. Twenty-four-year-old Melvin Wade had been convicted and sentenced to die for the rape of a childish black girl who was just twelve years of age when she was assaulted.

Dad told that Bessie Mae, clad in a pajama suit, had wept as she entered the execution chamber into which she had been accompanied by two prison matrons, the North Carolina prison chaplain and several guards. He related that the matrons seemed shaken and they clung to each other while watching the guards strap Bessie Mae into the chair in which she was about to die.

Earlier that morning, Bessie Mae told the ministers that she had spent the night praying and searching the scriptures, and that she felt ready to go. She voluntarily confessed to being one of the culprits at the scene of the crime and to lifting two half dollars that had fallen onto the cab seat. She, however, steadfastly denied taking part in the murder of the ill-fated driver.

Thompson told the visiting chaplains that he was ready to go prior to being taken from his cell. He admitted to being influenced by the devil but beyond that he offered no comment as to his role in the slaying. Someone told my father that Thompson had previously admitted to cutting the driver to death during the robbery. He, however, went silently to his death and he declined to make a final statement.

Dad stated that it had taken well over an hour to purge the toxic fumes from the chamber following the simultaneous executions of Bessie Mae Williams and Ralph Thompson, and then make it ready to take the life of Melvin Wade.

Wade, a Roman Catholic, had received the last rites of the Church only moments before he was taken into the execution chamber. A local priest had visited him several times during his confinement in the death house and had returned to administer the last rites of the Church on the morning of his execution. Wade told the chaplains and the visiting priest that he was ready to go and he had offered what dad described as a qualified denial of raping the twelve year old girl. Wade stated that, "I really am not guilty." Based on his experience with many inmates and the way they would construe words and meanings, Dad took that denial to mean that Wade had indeed had sex with the juvenile girl, but that the act was consensual.

The Long Train Ride Home

MY FATHER WAS GIVEN a ride to the train station by one of the ministers who had witnessed the executions, perhaps Chaplain Watts. They discussed the crimes for which the trio had been put to death as well as the brutality of the electric chair and the gas chamber. They said their farewells at the train depot and were never again in contact.

The train ride back to Columbia provided my father some time to contemplate his observations of the gas chamber executions and to ponder his answer to Governor Johnston.

He took the long New Year's weekend to pray and meditate over what he would tell the governor when he delivered his report during the first week of January 1945.

Governor Johnston, who had just resigned to take his seat in the United States Senate, listened attentively to Dad's description of the gas chamber executions. My father conveyed that one method of execution was about as agonizing as was the other. He felt the person being electrocuted was rendered instantly unconscious with the first surge of electrical current into the brain, but that it took much longer for those dying in the gas chamber to lose awareness.

To my father, it seemed those breathing the toxic fumes from the vats of acid placed beneath the execution chairs took some five to eight minutes to lose consciousness. Before succumbing, their breathing became tortured as they gulped for air and attempted to accelerate their death. Dad observed that it took over an hour to vent the deadly fumes, retrieve the body, and bring in the next person to be executed. By contrast, the electric chair required only minutes to inflict death, remove the body and made ready to repeat the procedure.

Due to my father's report, the governor decided against seeking to replace the electric chair as the means of execution in South Carolina. Johnston was a caring person, and his concern for the suffering of those whose lives were being taken was genuine.

My father often stated that the hardened criminal knew how to avoid the death penalty. He felt it was the less hardened individuals who would be executed for the same crime. The case of the North Carolina cab driver would seem to verify those views. Of the four people involved in the cabbies murder, three were in their teens. And the teen-aged Bessie Mae Williams and Ralph Thompson went to the gas chamber while fourteen-year-old Annie Mae Allison escaped death only because of her age. However, the hardened twenty-four-year old Cleve Johnson knew how to bargain a plea and escape the death penalty.

Chapter 11
Impulsive Charles Gilstrap

At the time of his arrest for the crime for which he was executed, Charles Gilstrap was a twenty-eight-year-old petty criminal with a long record of non-serious violations in his hometown of Greenville, South Carolina. He had been arrested at least eighteen times for minor offenses during a time span that began in November of 1937 and continued through December of 1943. He was thrice punished for possessing unlawful weapons but was never charged with using such weapons.

Police records reveal that he was arrested for the first time in the city of Greenville on November 19, 1937 for carrying a concealed handgun. That charge resulted in the largest penalty ever lodged against him for what became a pattern of petty offenses over the ensuing six years. The punishment for that violation was a fine of fifty-two dollars or thirty days in jail.

The very next day, Gilstrap was again arrested for concealing and carrying brass knucks. That infraction resulted in a fine of twenty-seven dollars or thirty days behind bars. Some four years later in November of 1941, he was arrested for the third and final time on a concealed weapons charge. That apprehension resulted in a sentence of thirty days or thirty dollars, the second largest penalty ever imposed on Charles Gilstrap. Several of his arrests were for offenses so minor in nature that the charges were dropped. Then, on February 4, 1944, in a manner that illustrated his impulsive nature, he committed the offense that sent him to the electric chair.

His prior detainments, other than the three arrests for carrying concealed weapons, were for such things as disorderly conduct, resisting arrest, public drunkenness, speeding, trespassing, or damaging private property. There is no doubt but that the poorly educated cab and truck driver, a school dropout who stood six feet tall and was of medium build, was a rowdy character. However, nothing in his arrests record would indicate that he was even remotely capable of committing the crime for which he was executed.

Gilstrap was not a man to back away from a brawl as was evidenced by his three arrests on various weapons charges. The knucks he carried were molded from brass, and were worn over the knuckles of a clenched fist. Their purpose was to enable the user to inflict serious injury on an opponent while engaged in the vicious barroom brawls that Gilstrap so loved.

His penchant to fight was validated by the ugly scars on his face and body. Some of those blemishes were no doubt the result of his many confrontations. And it is probable that brass knucks were the cause of some of those marks. In addition to the scars, Gilstrap was tattooed with symbols of women and seaside scenery on his arms, chest, shoulders and right leg.

However, this small-time street and tavern brawler acted totally out of character when, on February 4, 1944, he accosted and assaulted an eleven-year-old schoolgirl as she made her way home from a bus stop. His involvement was not planned or premeditated his actions were spontaneous. Nonetheless, for what turned out to be the final time he would act out on his impulses, he committed an intolerable act of sexual aggression against a juvenile girl, a capital offense that sent him to sit in the execution chamber.

Testimony revealed that on the Friday of the assault, Gilstrap began the day by meeting his wife in downtown Greenville to do some early morning shopping, following completion of her midnight shift at a nearby textile mill. They shopped until around eight-thirty before heading home where they arrived within a half hour. Gilstrap stayed with his spouse until around eleven o'clock before he became restless.

He then caught a bus back into town and met up with a pair of cronies that he described as "some boys." The trio did some heavy drinking in several sleazy establishments before deciding to visit a taxi stop where Gilstrap was employed. As they walked toward his work station, they consumed an additional half pint of whiskey. Gilstrap related that as they neared his place of work, that one of his companions headed off to his job and that his other intoxicated friend simply wandered away.

From the taxi stand, Gilstrap walked across the street to the bus depot where he boarded a bus that plied the city's Overbrook route. During the ride, the eleven-year-old girl, with school-books in hand, came aboard the transit vehicle and rode for a short distance before getting off. Gilstrap was inexplicably attracted to the preteen youngster, and, acting on impulse, he left the bus when she exited and followed her into a wooded area that provided a shortcut to her home.

The Crime and the Trial

WHILE ON THE WITNESS stand Gilstrap testified that he sidled up beside the girl and took her hand as they traversed the path through the trees. He stated that he began talking and that he asked her to stay with him for a few minutes after which he promised to let her go. She protested that her mother was sick and that she needed to get home to be with her parent.

Gilstrap told that they continued to talk and that, without protest, she agreed to go with him into the woods to a more isolated area. He testified that his passion was up and that he possessed an oversexed body. He also admitted to inserting his finger into her vagina as they lay on the ground together. The excitement of that act caused him to ejaculate, and he noticed that she had begun to emit a small amount of blood.

Gilstrap persistently denied making penile contact with her. He believed that if his penis was never inside her vagina, there was no way that he could be guilty of rape. And from the moment of his arrest, he readily admitted to his actions. However, he seemed incapable of grasping the seriousness of his latest offense.

The victim's testimony contradicted Gilstrap's version of their encounter, but she did corroborate some of his statement. She verified the transit ride and confirmed that he followed her into the woods from where she had exited the bus. From there, their accounts differ as to how the subsequent events developed. She told that when they reached the midway point along the trail, that he grabbed her from behind and said, "If you say anything, I will hurt you."

She told that he took her into the woods and that he pushed her to the ground while tearing off her pants. He then pulled his trousers down about halfway and got on top of her. The prosecuting attorney asked, "What did he do?" She replied, "Fucked me." The prosecutor then asked, "Did he say anything about what he was going to do?" She replied, "He said that he was going to fuck me."

The youngster stated that what he did was painful but they continued lying on the ground for about a half hour before getting up. Gilstrap pleaded with her not to tell anyone, and he left. She gathered her books and ran the rest of the way home to tell her mother of her ordeal with the unknown man. Her mother notified the police and rushed the child to the hospital.

Following the senseless assault, Gilstrap went back into town and got himself thoroughly drunk at a local cafe. He knew that he was in serious trouble but he made no attempt to flee. He drank into the early evening before returning home and going to sleep.

At around nine o'clock, he was awakened and pulled from the bed by police officers who were there to arrest him. The girl gave a detailed description of her attacker, and due to his lengthy police record as well as the tattoos and scars on his face and body, the authorities had little difficulty connecting Charles Gilstrap to the crime.

The girl and her mother came to police headquarters during the interrogation and the child identified Gilstrap as her attacker. He admitted to her accusations but refused to accept a plea bargain offer, an offer of life in prison in lieu of being tried for the rape of a minor. Perhaps the offer to make a plea was the authorities' attempt to spare the eleven-year-old from taking the witness stand if the case went to trial. However, Gilstrap would not cooperate. In his mind, without penile penetration, it was impossible for the charge of rape to stand up against him.

There is no way to know if the plea bargain offer was legitimate or if it was OK'd by the prosecutor who would determine the charges on which Gilstrap would be tried. Nonetheless, as much as Charles Gilstrap feared death in the chair, he should have risked a chance on that offer. The Miranda Warning rules were not in effect when Gilstrap was questioned. And without an attorney present, he probably forfeited his life during the interrogation.

Charles Gilstrap knew not that assault with intent was a capital offense that required only proof of intent to impose the death penalty. He failed to grasp that by rejecting the plea bargain that he was ignorantly gambling away his very own life to the electric chair.

He was tried in May following his crime in February. The no-nonsense jury in Greenville took but little time to reach a verdict and, on May 9, 1944, Charles Gilstrap was found guilty of the charges against him. The jury did not make a recommendation for mercy and the death sentence was mandatory. The death sentence was originally scheduled to be imposed on June 16, 1944. And except for his appeal to the South Carolina Supreme Court, Gilstrap would have joined fourteen-year-old George Stinney and Bruce Hamilton when they took their seats in the chair on that June morning.

Ironically, of the three men set to be executed on June 16, Bruce Hamilton and Charles Gilstrap were represented by the same attorney, John M. Schofield. Even though the cases were not related and all were tried in separate jurisdictions, all three men were sentenced to die on the same date, a date that only Gilstrap would fail to keep.

Some seven months following the original date set for Gilstrap's execution, the South Carolina Supreme Court rejected his appeal and upheld the sentence of the lower court. He was then scheduled to die on January 5, 1945. However, only days before the sentence were to be imposed, Governor Ransome J. Williams granted a stay of execution until February 9th. Williams, the former lieutenant governor, was elevated to the state's highest office when Olin D. Johnston resigned at the end of December 1944 to take his seat in the United States Senate.

Williams was the governor who would later declare that, "I would rather commute the sentences of ten who are guilty than to execute one who is innocent." Williams wanted time to review the case and to give attorney John Schofield an opportunity to prove that, even though the girl had been disgustingly molested, a lesser penalty was more appropriate for the impulsive Gilstrap. Charles Gilstrap did not rob gas stations or commit murder. He simply could not resist getting stoned and becoming involved in some vicious altercations. Gov. Williams wanted to be fair with those who stood condemned and because of that diligent attitude; Gilstrap was given a reprieve that would delay his doom for an additional thirty-five days.

During the month of reprieve, an element of religious support for Gilstrap began to emerge throughout the state. Church pastors wrote Governor Williams to plead for the life of the impulse-driven offender who claimed to have repented of his wicked ways. Ministers and other religious petitioners believed Gilstrap's declaration that he was repentant and that he wanted only to live out the remainder of his days as a servant of Jesus Christ.

The Reverend J. W. McLain, a Nazarene church pastor and close friend of my father's, visited the governor and pleaded for the life of the doomed Gilstrap before paying a call on the girl victim's father at his home in Greenville. Following his visit with Gov. Williams, McLain felt that the governor was prone to grant clemency if the parents offered no objection to the sentence being commuted. McLain was the father of two young daughters and was also regarded as a sincere and compassionate minister. And even though the reverend utilized his considerable ability to plead for the life of the doomed Gilstrap, the victim's father would not consent to a life sentence. Thus, the Rev. McLain's pleas were to no avail.

Gilstrap Pleads with the Governor

AS HIS DAYS TICKED away, Gilstrap twice wrote his own pleas for mercy. The first of his letters to Gov. Williams was dated January 31, 1945, with a follow-up letter dated February 4th. The letters were surprisingly articulate for the eighth-grade dropout. Even so, the letters were seen by Williams as shallow and unconvincing. Gilstrap's claim of conversion to Christianity and of regretting the life he had lived somehow failed to convince the governor of his sincerity.

Gilstrap acknowledged his guilt in the letters but continued to insist that he had not raped the child. Because of his dogged insistence that he was not a rapist, the governor took his words to be self-serving and not indicative of any measure of repentance. In one letter, Gilstrap implores the governor to believe that he would be a witness for Jesus and that he would be a force for good while serving life in the penitentiary. He begged that he wanted only to live out his days serving his Lord and Savior, Jesus Christ. He also informs that he is oversexed but that he had recently learned of an operation that would relieve his condition, and that he would gladly submit to castration if his life could be spared.

He further damaged his plea by telling that his attorney, John M. Schofield, had made passes at his wife and that Schofield was attempting to become the beneficiary of his life insurance policy. The young John Schofield was the same attorney who had waged a ceaseless battle to spare the life of Bruce Hamilton with whom Gilstrap had been scheduled to die on June 16, of the previous year.

Even as Gilstrap criticized Schofield, the lawyer pursued every means available to save the life of his client. With death staring him in the face, Gilstrap was willing to risk alienating his dedicated attorney, or say anything to escape sitting in the chair. The former macho-man was not afraid of the brain rattling knucks he encountered during many barroom brawls, but he was terrified of sitting in the electric chair.

Even though his client belittled him to the governor, the attorney would not give up the battle to change the deadly outcome. Having exhausted every legal means open to him, John Schofield then began a letter writing campaign in which he implored the governor to spare the life of Charles Gilstrap. In a message dated February 2, 1945, Schofield alluded to the possibility of castration if the life of his client could be spared. In the letter, Schofield lists five reasons why he believes a commutation of the death sentence is in order. The third reason given by the attorney is as follows:

> It has been a long time, if ever, that a white man has been electrocuted in South Carolina for rape. I have not checked the records and my memory does not go back many years, but I have checked with many older attorneys who state that they cannot remember where a white man was electrocuted on the charge of rape in this state. It is conceded by everyone that the purpose of the death penalty in rape cases, is to deal with the colored problem that

> we have in South Carolina. The main purpose is to
> hold down colored men attacking white women.

Ingrained racism was alive and well in South Carolina during the 1940s, and the black man's plight was at times deplorable. However, despite Schofield's words to the governor concerning "colored men attacking white women," it mattered not to the attorney whether his client was black or white. He took seriously his responsibility to defend them, and he used whatever means necessary. The young lawyer was not a racist and he fought just as hard for his black clients as he did for those who were white. That quality is illustrated in his defense of Bruce Hamilton in Chapter Eight.

Another reason listed in Schofield's appeal was the fragile health of Charles Gilstrap's mother. Schofield wrote that two of her sons were gravely ill, one of them near death in a Greenville hospital where he had been for several months. He told the governor that another of her sons was wasting away in a tuberculosis sanitarium. Schofield advised that the two sons would no doubt be dead within six months and that to execute Charles would be more than "this good Christian lady could bear." He argued that if Gilstrap were put to death, his ailing mother would be unable to endure the grief. He also expressed that no one would criticize the governor for such an act of kindness on behalf of this heartbroken old mother.

The letter also informed of improper and inflammatory conduct by the trial prosecutor. Schofield advised of some pertinent information concerning the alleged sexual behavior of the eleven-year-old that he had given to the state pardons and parole board for them to consider as they reviewed the case.

The fifth reason listed in attorney Schofield's no-stone-left-unturned appeal for executive clemency is as follows:

> The fifth reason that I wish to submit in
> my contention for a commutation is that the

seriousness of the crime of rape is in the taking of virtue from a woman. If the virtue is lacking before the crime then the seriousness of the crime is less. There is some evidence that in spite of this girl's youth she was not virtuous. This can be seen by reading the file which is in the hands of the Pardon Board.

Whether one admires or loathes the tenacity with which Attorney John Schofield defended his clients, it should be recognized that each and every one of his defendants got the very best legal representation that the young lawyer was capable of giving. And until the morning of their execution the unflinching attorney battled to save them.

Charles Gilstrap is executed

GOVERNOR WILLIAMS, AFTER CAREFUL consideration of the pleas, refused to grant a commutation of the death sentence, and on the morning of February 9, 1945, Charles Gilstrap was strapped securely into the chair to pay with his life for the only known serious crime he had ever committed.

As Gilstrap entered the death chamber, he was visibly shaken. He trembled noticeably, and, Dr. M. Whitfield Cheatham, the prison physician, took notice of the shaking Gilstrap. In a kindly attempt to calm the nerves of the doomed inmate, the doctor commented: "It sure is cold in here this morning." That observation drew a concurring reaction from the fear stricken Gilstrap, who responded, "Yes, it is very cold." He was then strapped into the chair and asked if he wished to make a final statement. He responded with a lengthy discourse that was reported by *The Columbia Record* in their edition dated February 9, 1945:

I want to thank the guards for treating me well and, as far as I know and to the best of my knowledge, I have been saved by the blood of Jesus Christ. I'm sorry for what I done. I don't blame the people for thinking of me as they do. I do not think I got justice but I am ready to meet God. I'm going to a place where I am going to get justice.

Looking upward, he said, "God, I hope you'll keep looking on me. I am going to see God in just a few minutes."

My father visited him twice on the day before his execution. While there, Dad met various members of the family who were visiting. They included his wife, mother, brother, and other relatives who stayed until late that Thursday evening. Dad, accompanied by the Reverend C. F. Wimberly, also visited for an hour on the final morning and right up until the condemned man was led from his cell into the death chamber.

Gilstrap's brother visited on the morning of the execution and it was only an hour before Charles was put to death that the two brothers bid each other an emotional farewell. The sibling then left the death house to rejoin the grief-stricken family, where they waited to escort the body to their hometown of Easley for burial.

Approximately seventy-five people, including two young women, were present to witness the Gilstrap execution. And immediately prior to his entry into the death chamber, the prison superintendent found it necessary to demand quietness and remind the male observers to remove their hats as a gesture of respect for the life that was to be taken.

Gilstrap became the second inmate put to death during the 1940s to be interred in the small town of Easley, a community where violent crime was uncommon. However, due to the behavior of J. C. Hann in Chapter One, and Charles Gilstrap, the little cotton mill hamlet became the final resting place for that pair of native sons who had misbehaved so badly.

Attorney Schofield Complimented

GOVERNOR WILLIAMS, IN RESPONSE to Schofield's letter on behalf of Gilstrap, complimented the young lawyer for his diligent defense and stated that he admired him for having done his very best to spare the life of his client. He told Schofield that he would like to meet him, and he invited the attorney to come for a visit at the governor's office the next time he was in Columbia.

Governor Olin D. Johnston had also written a complimentary letter in praise of Attorney Schofield for the battle he had waged on behalf of Bruce Hamilton, who was executed in June of 1944.

AUTHOR'S NOTE: LAWYER SCHOFIELD was mistaken when he alleged that no white man had been executed for rape in the state of South Carolina. As is illustrated in Chapter One, the Evans brothers and their cousin, Hampton Lee, all of them white, were executed in February of 1941 following their conviction for the rape of a young Caucasian woman in the late summer of 1940.

Chapter 12
George Carter

G eorge Carter was twenty-nine years of age and Christmas was only eleven days away when he took his seat in the chair on December 14, 1945. Despite the joy of the season for those of the Christian faith, in which Carter affirmed his belief, he would not be around to enjoy the small measure of celebration allowed at the penal institution on Christmas Day. The practice was to allow a day of relief from the intense work routine and, the boring diet was substituted with a traditional offering of turkey and dressing for the Yule Day meal. The inmates looked forward to the holiday menu and the day off from work when many would receive what was their once yearly visit from friends and relatives.

Unfortunately for the wiry George Carter, who stood five feet, four inches tall and weighed less than one hundred and thirty pounds, his date with the executioner would not wait for him to enjoy the holiday. Carter was serving a forty-year sentence as a trustee on the Greenville County chain gang when he committed the crime that sent him to the chair. He was convicted of criminal assault with intent to ravish a middle-aged, married woman who he knew by sight, and she recognized him as her assailant. Nothing found in our research indicated that the woman was Caucasian. However, since Carter was black and was sentenced on the charge of assault with intent to ravish, it is virtually certain that his victim was white. Several black youths were executed for their conviction on that charge during the segregated 1940s.

Carter denied the charge and steadfastly declared his innocence to my father and Chaplain E. A. Davis throughout his nineteen-day stay in the death house. Dad said that he was calm during his final days and that he showed no fear when he was strapped into the chair. He did, however, before leaving his cell reaffirm his Christian belief while steadfastly denying any guilt.

Carter was married but it is not known if he had children. His wife corresponded with him during his incarceration at the prison but did not visit during his almost three weeks of confinement in the death house. However, she and his relatives did claim the body and took it back home for burial.

Ironically, both Judge J. H. Johnson, who imposed the death sentence at the conclusion of the trial, and George Carter were from the same hometown of Allendale. Prior to his conviction on the earlier offense for which he was serving a forty-year sentence, a sexual assault that was similar to the transgression for which he was executed, Carter had farmed a plot in the area near Simpsonville. His sentence was imposed on the last day of October 1945. And in that era when the rendering of justice was seldom delayed, in just six weeks he was executed on the morning of December 14.

Morning of the Execution

REPORTER MARK WARREN COVERED the execution, and his report was published in the *Columbia Record* dated December 14, 1945. Excerpts are as follows:

Prior to his entrance into the death room, Colonel J. S. Wilson, penitentiary superintendent, asked all spectators, numbering some 70 persons, including two young white women, to remove their hats.

After Carter was seated, Assistant Captain Claude A. Sullivan asked Carter if he had a statement.

"No sir," Carter replied distinctly.

"Nothing?" Captain Sullivan remarked.

Carter, who had his eyes closed, apparently in prayer, did not reply.

Dr. M. Whitfield Cheatham, attending physician who stood nearby, asked Carter again, after the straps were adjusted, if he wanted to offer any statement. Carter did not reply but merely shook his head in the negative fashion.

A few minutes prior to leaving his cell in the death house, Carter told the Reverend E. A. Davis, pastor of the Bethlehem Baptist Church, that he was innocent of the charge.

Earlier, he told the Reverend C. M. Kelly and Dr. Charles F. Wimberly, also, that he was not guilty as charged.

"I had a nice rest last night," Carter was quoted as saying.

The chaplain observed that Carter was calm on every occasion he visited him in his cell.

Prior to leaving his death house cell, Carter made a profession as to his belief in Christianity.

None of Carter's relatives were present, nor were any relatives of the attempted assault victim, a middle-aged married woman from the Marietta community in Greenville County, prison attaches said.

The state electrician, Sam Cannon, reported that Carter's death occurred within 3 minutes and 44 seconds after the current was turned on by the electric chair switch.

He first applied 2,300 volts for five seconds, followed by reduced voltage of 1,400—the usual method. It appeared that Carter died on the first application, as he jerked upward violently. Death was pronounced by Doctor Cheatham.

"I'm ready to meet God," was one of Carter's last remarks prior to his last walk from his cell to the nearby electric chair, prison attaches said.

Among the spectators today were about 10 Negroes, some of them prison trustees.

Two representatives of a Greenville funeral home were present and removed the body to that city. They said it had been claimed by relatives, but that the funeral had not been arranged.

Upon conclusion of the execution, Sgt. C. Wardlaw Moorman of the prison staff had 10 witnesses sign the papers as to the execution, one copy of which will be sent to the clerk of courts of Greenville County.

Chapter 13
Wash Pringle

The execution of Wash Pringle, a thirty-two-year-old black man from Sumter County, was, in my father's opinion, another of the executions imposed during his prison ministry where he felt the defendant was innocent of the charge or that the death sentence was excessive for the crime committed.

Pringle was convicted for the rape of a white woman in Sumter County following his one day trial on November 16, 1945. The alleged violation had occurred on a lonely stretch of road during the wee morning hours of October 23 of that same year. And, an all-white male jury required only ninety minutes of deliberations to find Pringle guilty of the alleged offense that sent him to the electric chair.

The presiding judge, J. Woodrow Lewis, set the execution date for December 21, a date that was less than three full months following the alleged crime, and only five weeks subsequent to Pringle's conviction. Governor Ransome J. Williams, as was his nature, wanted time to review the case personally before allowing the execution. And because of the governor's diligence, Pringle was granted a stay of execution.

On November 17, 1945, the Sumter Daily News, in a terse, four-paragraph article, reported that Pringle had been convicted of the rape and sentenced to death. Few details of the crime were provided except that "the crime allegedly occurred on a highway in Sumter County in the early morning of October 23." Details of the assault were not reported. And such an absence of news coverage was an unusual situation when a white woman was assaulted by a black man during the 1940s. Such crimes typically received ongoing and extensive news publicity by the press and on local radio broadcasts.

Pringle went to the death house on December 2, just two weeks following his conviction on November 17. However, due to Gov. Williams' decision to stay the sentence until late January of 1946, it was necessary to move Pringle to Cellblock F, death row, for several of the intervening weeks. Otherwise, the authorities would have violated the statute that prohibited doomed inmates from spending more than twenty days in the death house.

During Pringle's incarceration, my dad and Chaplain E. A. Davis visited him frequently. And my father visited him every day and sometimes twice daily following his transfer to the death house. Pringle always denied being guilty of anything more than having consensual sex with his alleged victim. And he declared that their involvement on the day of his arrest was just one of many rendezvous in their ongoing affair.

He explained that the woman's husband had gotten knowledge of their dates and that he had waited for them to meet again. When the two did meet during the early morning hours of October 23 for another of their forbidden trysts, the husband had knowledge of their plan. He then notified the sheriff's office to provide details for when and where the pair could be caught in the act. According to Pringle, when the officers arrived at the roadside spot where the two were having sex, in order to save her reputation and her marriage, his willing partner accused him of rape. Of course, since the arresting officers witnessed them having sex, they knew that Wash Pringle was indeed with the married woman, and they accepted her word that the act was forced upon her.

Wash would show his softer side to my father during the chaplains' many visits. He talked about his four "poor little children" and of having to die and leave them without a father. Tears would flow as he told about his kids and his faithful wife. He seemed truly repentant and honest when pouring out his heart and soul to either of the two chaplains.

Wash Pringle's wife claimed the body and had it returned to Sumter County for interment in the Beulah Church Cemetery. One cannot but try and imagine the visceral pain and suffering, the agony that was felt by his faithful spouse and their four small children as the family watched his coffin being lowered into the ground. The children, who were adored by both parents, were the true victims of their father's immoral behavior. His was the behavior that took him away from them during the years that they and their mom needed him most.

My father found it difficult to talk about his experience with Wash Pringle, his spouse and his children. His heart was broken over the plight of the faithful wife and her pathetic brood of children, youngsters who could not fully comprehend the tragedy that came into their lives.

The *Columbia Record*, dated January 25, 1946, published the events of the execution that morning. Following are excerpts from the article by reporter Mark Warren:

> Wash Pringle, 32, died today in the electric chair at the state penitentiary death house and in his last words asked God to show mercy on him.

> After guards led Pringle to the execution room, Assistant Capt. Claude A. Sullivan of the guard staff asked Pringle if he had anything to say.

> "No sir, I've nothing to say... May God have mercy on me."

The Rev. Davis (chaplain) said Pringle told him just before he left his cell to die in the chair that he was innocent of the charge against him.

Sgt. C. Wardlaw Moorman of the prison office staff said, "Pringle's relatives had visited him frequently. His wife and four children made their last trip to the prison yesterday."

State electrician, Sam Cannon applied the current for three minutes and forty-one seconds, starting out with 2300 volts, and giving successively 1350 and 600 volts. Dr. M. Whitfield Cheatham, prison physician, pronounced Pringle dead at the end of that time.

The article also told that Pringle was the 268th person to die in the chair since the first man was electrocuted on August 6, 1912.

Chapter 14
Louis C. Gatlin

====================

Louis Gatlin was an enlisted black soldier from the bucolic little town of Biloxi on the Gulf Coast of Mississippi. He had grown up in that area of white sand beaches and natural beauty but seemed unaware of the Mississippi that so elicits those poignant yet nostalgic mental images of plantations, cotton fields, mule-drawn wagons, shotgun shacks and the fragrance of magnolia trees in blossom. Instead, Louis Gatlin smarted from the poverty and the indignities that were the lot of his people throughout the states of Dixie.

Louis Gatlin was an angry young man who, by his own admission, hated the white race of human beings. And that turmoil from deep within Louis Gatlin boiled from its caldron on the night of March 31, 1945 to trigger the rape of an innocent young white woman, the wife of a fellow soldier who was off fighting Hitler's Nazi armies in Europe. Not only did the young victim suffer the ordeal of Gatlin's fury, Louis Gatlin himself would undergo the humiliation of having his own life snuffed out as compensation for his crime.

At the time of the attack, Gatlin was stationed at the Charleston port of embarkation from where the Army shipped its troops to the fighting fronts of Western Europe. For reasons that are unknown and perhaps not understood by Louis Gatlin himself, his loathing of the white man erupted under a radiant March moon and culminated in one of the more brutal rapes in the long history of South Carolina. His was a vicious crime in which he seemed driven to inflict as much degradation on his blameless victim as he possibly could.

The Evening of the Attack

THE POLICE INVESTIGATION, IMMEDIATELY following the assault, established that the twenty-four-year-old woman had been shopping in downtown Charleston. From there she had taken a bus out to a stop in the city's suburbs that was a long block from where she lived. She departed the bus at approximately 10:30 p.m. and began the short walk to the apartment home that was shared with her mother.

She left the sidewalk from where she had exited the bus to cross some railroad tracks that ran parallel to the road. From the sidewalk she took a footpath that angled away from the road but served as a shortcut to her home. She told that she was unaware of anyone in the area until after having walked a few steps along the foot path, she heard a noise from behind that sounded as if someone had run from the thicket and jumped onto the sidewalk. She was not particularly alarmed but she did turn to see the cause of the commotion. And she saw a black man dressed in soldier's khaki, wearing an overseas cap, running towards her.

He ran up and grabbed her right shoulder just as she reached a secondary rail track that she also had to cross before reaching home. The youth stared at her for a second and she let out a scream. He said, "Woman I am going to fuck you." She then began "hollering" for her mother, who was at home, sick in bed.

She told that he shoved her down on the tracks and that while kneeling over her that he forced her hand up to cover her mouth and nose. She narrated that a man was walking on the sidewalk and that he almost touched them when he passed, but that he did not hear her muffled plea for help. Once the man was gone, Gatlin grabbed her by the hair, pulled her to her feet, and dragged her backwards into a thicket on the opposite side of the tracks. She avowed that she was "fighting like the devil" while being dragged by the hair and "boxed in the face." She was again thrown to the ground and while lying on her back, she managed to kick him in the chest. The kick did nothing but infuriate him even more than he already was, and he resumed punching her face until they heard voices talking on the nearby sidewalk. Upon hearing the voices, he ceased "boxing her face" and grabbed a stick from the ground. He placed it against her eye and whispered that he would punch out her eyes if she screamed. She conveyed that he also picked up a rock and threatened her with a gun. However, she told that she never saw a gun.

The police learned that once the pedestrians on the sidewalk were gone, the assailant ripped off her clothes and with her lying naked on the ground, he pulled down his pants and assaulted her "in every way imaginable." She was too physically exhausted to resist, and he forced himself on her three times. When finished with the repeated acts of copulation, he threatened her with death. He tore the watch from her wrist and then began urinating on her nude body while asking if she had any money. She replied that she had no money, and he responded, "You are a god damn liar." She stated, however, that he made no attempt to retrieve her purse or check to see if she was lying about having no money, even though the bag was only a few feet from where they lay.

Even after three sexually penetrating assaults, he was not finished and once more he thrust himself brutally into her. In desperation for him to finish she pleaded that her mother was sick and that she needed to get home to care for her parent. He replied, "God damn your people, I think I will kill you right here." He then raped her again and again. Once during the brutal process he asked, "Do you hate Negroes?" She stated, "I knew better than to answer yes."

He told her that his name was John Bale. He then forced her to hold his penis as he kissed her lips and stuck his tongue in her mouth. However, he was startled when she asked if they could meet again the following night at the same place, a question that prompted him to end the assault. Her query appeared to whet his anger and every time she opened her mouth to continue talking, he would draw back his fist as if to strike her again. Several moments following her offer to meet again, he told her to look the other way and he took off running down the tracks.

The frantic young victim scrambled to cover her nakedness and with blackened eyes, bruised and swollen features, she scooped up her belongings and hurried home. Her parent rendered first aid and rushed to get her ready to be taken to the nearby Stark Hospital. A neighbor, a sergeant in the military owned a car and had offered to drive them. A pair of soldiers was passing on the street and the sergeant asked them to phone the Charleston police.

The soldiers called and law enforcement officers were dispatched to meet the victim at the emergency room to hear her account of what had transpired. The young woman gave an excellent explanation of the attack as well as an accurate description of the man who assaulted her. However, due to her injuries, she could not return home and was admitted to the hospital. There she would spend the first six days of her many weeks of recovery.

While convalescing at the infirmary, a hospital provided car took her to see a suspect who was arrested on April 2, 1945. Detectives felt the detainee was her assailant, but they needed her to identification him. She remembered the moon shone brightly on the night of her ordeal and that she had gotten several clear looks at the features of her rapist. Immediately upon viewing the man in custody, she identified Louis C. Gatlin as her attacker.

Trial Date is Set

IT SHOULD BE NOTED that conflicting opinions were presented before Judge William H. Grimball of the Ninth Judicial Circuit by both the prosecutor, Robert Mc C. Figg Jr., and Louis Gatlin's court appointed attorney, D. R. Stack, a Charleston lawyer.

In a pre-trial argument, Stack sought to quash the indictment because there had been no blacks on the grand jury that returned the true bill and not a single person of the "Negro" race was present to serve on the petit jury venire for the week beginning June 11, 1945, the week the trial was to begin. Judge Grimball rejected the request and the trial got under way on June 14.

The Trial Begins

THE VICTIM TOOK THE witness stand and in response to a question by the prosecutor, she pointed to Gatlin who was seated with his attorney as the Negro soldier who attacked and raped her, trial records show. She also identified the watch that was wrenched from her wrist during the assault when it was offered as evidence.

Gatlin's commanding officer, an Army captain, then took the stand and testified that the watch was in Gatlin's personal belongings when his living quarters was searched at the time of his arrest.

A young, black enlistee, one of Gatlin's fellow soldiers also took the witness stand to be questioned and offer testimony.

The army private affirmed that he and his girlfriend were standing inside a restaurant on Coming Street, and preparing to play the piccolo, when Gatlin entered the eatery on a Sunday evening. He shared that Gatlin came up to them and admired the watch on the wrist of his lady friend. And, that Gatlin had pulled a similar timepiece from his pocket. The soldier described the watch they were shown as having a broken band. He said that Gatlin explained the watch was damaged while playing around with his girlfriend and that he was taking it to be repaired. The soldier also noted that the crystal was not in the timepiece when Gatlin showed it to him. He related that he saw the watch again when it was among Gatlin's personal possessions at the time of his arrest.

Additional testimony by the rape victim established that she continued visiting the hospital on a regular basis for two months following the assault. And that even at the time of the trial, some ten weeks following her terrifying ordeal, she was not fully recovered.

She proved credible as a witness and her courtroom narrative was consistent with what she told the police on the night she was questioned in the hospital. Her own and other testimony, coupled with overwhelming evidence against Gatlin, was convincing. Following testimony, it took an all-white jury only seventeen minutes to hold their deliberations and return a verdict of guilty against Louis Gatlin, the hate-filled soldier from Mississippi.

Judge Grimball set the date of execution for just a few weeks following the trial. But due to Attorney Stack's appeal of the sentence, in addition to a stay of execution granted by Gov. Williams, Gatlin was not to sit in the chair until the morning of July 19, 1946.

On July 20, the Charleston *News and Courier* printed an Associated Press dispatch on Gatlin's execution the previous morning. According to the article, Gatlin feigned insanity during the trial and was frequently heard muttering to himself, and he was occasionally seen beating on himself. The article also revealed that Gatlin had been examined by six psychiatrists at the state hospital and that after thirty days under psychiatric observation, he had been declared sane.

The article further stated that Gatlin told my father that he had slept some during the night and that he had made it right with his God. Gatlin had eaten a big chicken dinner the night before he was executed, and approximately twenty people were present when Gatlin was put to death, according to the newspaper. The news report also told that the body was claimed and that an undertaker was transporting it back to Gatlin's native Mississippi for burial.

Louis Gatlin, by his own death house admission to my father and Chaplain E. A. Davis, affirmed his guilt for one of the most brutal rapes that anyone could possibly imagine.

Chapter 15
Charles T. Smith, Cop Killer from Berkeley County

C harles T. Smith, an ageing black man, was electrocuted on the morning of November 29, 1946. He was sixty-six years of age and the oldest person electrocuted during my father's years as chaplain. Smith was put to death for the killing of a white law enforcement officer, W. Calhoun Guerry, after Guerry had placed him under arrest on May 25 of that same year. The small community of Jamestown, in Berkeley County, was the site of the slaying.

Extensive research uncovered but few news reports or official records of the crime and the execution of Charlie Smith. Even the *Columbia Record*, a daily publication that reported most crimes and executions in a very thorough manner, used only five brief paragraphs to cover the electrocution of the elderly Smith.

While little is known of the felony or the details of his trial, we do know that the wheels of justice spun a bit more slowly for Smith than it did for many of those executed during the 1940s. As is related in other chapters, many times the perpetrators of capital offenses were tried, sentenced, and executed within three to four months following the date on which they had committed their capital transgression. Somehow, even though the reasons for the delay are vague and his victim was a police officer, Charlie Smith was not tried until October following the murder of patrolman Guerry in May.

Smith was found guilty and sentenced to death on October 25, exactly five months following the slaying. Smith's reason for killing the officer is unknown to the author. However, once the judgement was passed, he was transferred to the death house on the fifteenth day following his sentencing and he was executed just a month and four days after learning his fate. Justice did indeed come swiftly during the 1940s.

The Judge Pronounces Sentence

> The prisoner at the bar, Charlie T. Smith, is to be conveyed hence to the County jail of the County of Berkeley, there to be kept in close and safe confinement, until he shall thence be conveyed to the State Penitentiary, as required by law, there to be kept in close and safe confinement, until Friday, November 29th, 1946, between the hours of five o'clock in the forenoon thereof and the hour of five o'clock in the afternoon thereof, upon which day, and between which hours, you, the prisoner at the bar, Charlie T. Smith, shall suffer death by electrocution at the hands of the officers of the law, and in the manner provided by the laws of the State of South Carolina, and may God have mercy on your soul.
>
> J. Frank Eatmon
> Presiding Judge
> Moncks Corner, S. C., October 25, 1946

Transferred to Death House

IN ACCORDANCE WITH THE sentence and with no motion filed for an appeal, Smith was taken to the maximum security prison in Columbia on November 10 and was immediately placed in the death house where he would live out the remaining nineteen days of his life.

My father, per his custom, visited Smith at least daily and often twice daily once he was confined in the death house. Most of those among the doomed sufferers appreciated my dad's visits and they reacted favorably to his concern for their being right with God. Smith, however, was unresponsive and he seemed disinterested in what either of the two penitentiary chaplains had to say. He was not impressed by their concerns over where he would spend eternity.

Smith, who was only five feet, four inches in height, and just one hundred and eleven pounds in weight, would not stand erect to talk with the chaplains. When singly, or sometimes jointly, the clergymen would pay their visits to him, he would rise from the cot on which he was reclining and come to the front of the cell. There, behind the steel mesh screen and iron bars, he would squat down to where his buttocks almost touched the concrete floor, and he would rock back and forth for the duration of their visits. From that position, he would seem to listen but rarely would he offer more than a yes or no in response to a question. He simply refused to engage any member of the clergy in conversation.

Smith was the oldest individual put to death during the years my father served as lead chaplain. And he was perhaps the oldest person ever electrocuted by the state of South Carolina. Most of those who were put to death in the electric chair during my fathers' tenure were in their late teens or early twenties. However, fourteen-year-old George Stinney Jr. was easily the least mature of the youths who were executed.

It is unknown to the author if the death sentence was disproportionately imposed on the younger offenders or whether the youthful transgressors committed the more serious violations in disproportionate numbers. However, it was the younger criminals who far more frequently received the death sentence for their acts of violence than did their older counterparts.

The *Columbia Record* published a brief account of the Smith execution in their afternoon edition dated November 29, 1946. The brief account of the execution by reporter Mark Warren is as follows:

> Showing no trace of emotion and expressing no regret for the slaying which led to his death sentence, Charles T. Smith, 66-year-old Berkeley County Negro, died quietly today in the electric chair at the state penitentiary.
>
> "I have nothing to say," he commented when Capt. Claude A. Sullivan of the prison staff asked him if he wanted to make any comment.
>
> State electrician, Sam Cannon, then proceeded with the execution, and Dr. M. Whitfield Cheatham, prison physician, pronounced Smith dead.
>
> The small death house, located in the main prison yard, was well filled with spectators, including several relatives of the late W. Calhoun Guerry, who was slain at Jamestown last May 25 after he had placed Smith under arrest.
>
> Smith was literally "a forgotten man" at the prison for unlike most condemned prisoners he had none of the usual visits from people from his home section, and today no one claimed his body.

Smith's burial was conducted after the execution in the little prison cemetery for those unclaimed persons, where around 100 persons are said to be buried.

Chapter 16
The Hot-Tempered Murderer
Junius A. Judge

T he case of Junius A. Judge qualifies as one of the more senseless murders in the history of the Palmetto State. The crime was spontaneous and over the slightest of disagreements between a bus driver and a hot-tempered passenger, Junius A. Judge.

Trial testimony established that Judge and a female companion boarded a South Carolina Power Company bus, a public transportation vehicle that was driven by Alric A. Gore. Records indicate that the bus stopped at Charleston's Milo Five Station where a number of "colored passengers" entered. The boarding passengers included Junius A. Judge and his girl companion.

When the doors closed and the vehicle began to move, someone standing on the sidewalk called out something to one of the passengers sitting inside the bus. It is not known what was said but the passenger inside responded: "Catch the next bus and come on." And, just after the large vehicle began to move, someone rang the alert bell to signal that they wanted to get off at the next stop.

Upon traveling the short distance to the next place for passengers to exit, driver Alric Gore halted the vehicle to let several commuters depart through the rear door. With the bus idling for those riders to leave, Judge and his girlfriend came forward to the driver and said, "We are not going any further. I want my money back." The driver allegedly replied, "I can't give you a dern cent back." Whereupon the "colored man" pulled out a revolver and shot the bus driver. That mindless and unprovoked shooting happened at around nine o'clock on the evening of April 16, 1945.

Witnesses told that the assailant and his female companion jumped from the bus and fled into the night as the driver lay mortally wounded, to die within minutes.

Testimony of what transpired was offered by a pair of passengers who were seated near the front of the vehicle and had an unobstructed view of the violent episode. They heard the verbal exchange between Judge and Gore. And each told that the driver had done absolutely nothing to provoke the deadly attack.

Neither of the witnesses could, however, identify Judge as the assailant. Nonetheless, when he was arrested on April 18, two days following the shooting, he held a loaded handgun. And the bullets in his pistol matched the pellet used to kill Alric Gore. Judge never denied the shooting and he admitted to slaying the driver with a cartridge that was identical to those found in his weapon. However, he had a different version of the words exchanged between him and the driver.

Judge testified that when he asked for the refund, the driver said, "Hell, no," and that he reached down and came up with a pistol. According to Judge, he and Gore fired their weapons in unison but only his shot hit its target. He told that the driver's shot grazed his head but that he escaped being injured.

Judge confirmed the events of the altercation and of firing the fatal shot when he was apprehended. However, eyewitness testimony contradicted Judge's claim that the driver had reached for a handgun, and no such weapon was ever found.

Junius Judge was indicted in June of 1945 for the murder of Alric Gore in April of that same year. He was tried within weeks and following a speedy trial and a brief period of jury deliberations, the panel rendered its verdict of guilty without a recommendation for mercy. Judge William H. Grimball then set the date of execution for August 1, 1945. Judge was transferred immediately to the maximum security penitentiary in Columbia to be confined on Cellblock –F, death row. There he awaited transfer to the death house and his appointment with the executioner. However, he was not to die on that date.

His lawyers refused to abandon the impulsive youth, as was so often the circumstance in that bygone era. They began a determined though futile struggle to alter the outcome with an immediate appeals to the South Carolina Supreme Court, which stayed the death sentence.

Judge remained on death row awaiting the outcome of his appeal and throughout his eleven months of confinement in those maximum security cells he never showed emotion nor did he ever express any sense of remorse for the murder.

Following the high court's decision not to overturn the verdict, Judge was immediately taken to Charleston on June 18, 1946, to be resentenced. His execution date was set for July 12, following which he taken back to the state penitentiary in Columbia and directly to the death house to wait the days until his execution. Fifteen months elapsed from the day of his crime until he was executed, and that was a very long time for justice to be rendered during that era.

My father and Chaplin E. A. "Lester" Davis stopped frequently during Judge's months on death row. And their visits became daily when he was moved to the death house, an area of six cells that were reminiscent of the cages used to house dangerous animals. The bleak death house conditions, however, were not meant for beastly predators. Those cells were there to confine predatory human beings who had inflicted pain and suffering on fellow human beings.

Judge was sullen by nature and he shared few if any of his thoughts with either of the chaplains. My father was unaware of

Judge having ever voiced any feeling of penitence. He seemed not to care that the driver was an hourly employee with no authority to grant refunds or to handle policy complaints by unhappy passengers. And he appeared to have established in his own mind that the driver was responsible for the situation over which he was slain.

On the morning of July 12, 1946, Judge was strapped securely into the chair where executioner, Sam Cannon, threw the switch to send twenty-three hundred volts of current surging into the brain of the man who had committed murder over a disputed bus fare. His grieving parents stood by him throughout the ordeal. And they claimed the body for burial.

Judge Family Problems

IT IS IRONIC THAT sixteen-year-old Matthew Judge, a cousin to Junius, had also been sentenced to die on August 1, 1945 for an unrelated crime in a different jurisdiction. Then, only weeks following Matthew having received the death sentence, his older relative Junius was sentenced to death on that same date.

Even though the cousins' were tried on varied dates for dissimilar crimes in separate jurisdictions, the presiding judge at each trial, William H. Grimball, pronounced the sentences and set August 1 as the date for each of the Judge cousins' to be executed. Unlike Junius whose action was spontaneous. Matthew plotted his attempt to rape a young white woman.

Appeals stayed the sentences and neither man died on the date set by Judge Grimball. However, for several months during the fall months of 1945 and well into 1946, the Judge cousins were confined simultaneously as condemned prisoners awaiting execution.

The mentally challenged Matthew was from Berkley County and his grandmother was listed as his next of kin. And he eventually escaped execution because of his mental retardation. Junius was not so fortunate! And he paid with his life for his mindless moment of outrage against a man who was only doing his job, as he was required to do it.

Then a youth of fifteen, I accompanied my father to visit Matthew in the death house. I hold a graphic memory of my dad pushing a pack of Juicy Fruit gum through the steel mesh into the hands of a smiling Matthew. Due to his dire condition, a pack of gum made him very happy.

Chapter 17
Gullah-Speaking Lewis Scott

L ewis Scott was a twenty-year-old black youth who admittedly had no one to blame but himself for his execution on December 20, 1946. Had he stayed sober and complied with the instructions of his police officer victim to stay out of town when rowdy and drunk, he would have averted the murderous confrontation with Officer Walter Evans. Evans, the night patrolman in Greeleyville was killed during a confrontation with Scott on September 14, 1945. And some fifteen months following the stupid slaying, Scott was strapped securely into the chair and had his life taken for that moment of drunken folly.

Cultural Background

GREELEYVILLE IS A SMALL crossroads town that was named in honor of the legendary newspaperman, Horace Greeley. The town is located in the farm belt of the Carolina low country where traces of the Gullah dialect can be heard in the words and speech patterns of those who are native to that region.

Gullah combines words and phrases from both the French and English languages that were spoken by the first Europeans to settle the area. Mingled among those languages are words and expressions derived from West African dialects that were spoken by the plantation slaves who toiled in the heat and oppressive humidity that is common to that region.

Scott spoke an eroded version of the Gullah dialect and he was a product of that hard farm environment of sweat and manual labor. Those who performed the backbreaking endeavors were known to booze it up and, at times, become quite rowdy. Scott came to rely on alcohol to dull the edge of his grueling life and he was prone to heavy drinking, a habit that often caused him to turn violent and, even deadly on that mid-September night in 1945.

Scott Commits Murder

ON THE DAY PRECEDING the shooting, Officer Evans had ordered Scott to leave town for being drunk and disorderly. Perhaps he should have placed him under arrest but the officer no doubt viewed him as a harmless drunk who would go home and sober up. Officer Evans obviously had no desire to arrest the intoxicated Scott and cause him to spend time in jail or be assessed a fine for being drunk and belligerent.

Even though ordered to stay out of town when drunk, Scott returned the following evening and he was spoiling for a fight. He told my father that as he staggered drunkenly along the street, he was spotted by the officer who came to place him under arrest. He said that he had been drinking heavily and did not immediately realize that the police officer was dead, or that he had killed him. Scott did, however, admit his guilt to my father.

On the afternoon of December 20, 1946, the *Columbia Record* published a report of the execution by reporter Mark Warren. Excerpts from the news article stated:

> Calm and collected and apparently willing to expiate for the murder of a Greeleyville policeman, 20-year-old Lewis Scott died quietly today in the electric chair at the state prison's death house.

Wearing a spotlessly white shirt and green-blue trousers, Scott walked into the death chamber unassisted and sat down showing no emotion, as he was strapped in the chair.

"Do you have anything you want to say?" asked Claude A. Sullivan of the penitentiary staff.

"Yes," Scott replied clearly.

Trusting In the Lord

"I can say this, that all the men, the sergeant, the captain, have been very nice to me in here and treated me very well. I am trusting in the Lord, and believe he will save me. The Lord has forgiven me for my sins."

Just before the death mask was placed over his face, Scott was heard to pray and say, aloud, "O God, be with me."

Two pastors, prison chaplains, the Rev. C. M. Kelly and the Rev. Edward A. Davis, were on duty early in the prison today to be with the condemned man.

"Everything is all right, I'm ready to meet the Lord," he told the Rev. Mr. Kelly.

The Rev. Davis carried Scott's Bible, which he gave him a week ago as a final token.

Death House Songs

The death house today in the cellblocks rang with religious music as one of the other occupants, Rose Marie Stinette, 41, of Lake City, awaiting execution next month for the murder of her husband, Charles, 39, who was bludgeoned to death at Florence, sang.

The other death house occupants, Roy Singletary, 22, held in the same death, and Cleve Covington, 26, of Clio, held in the murder of a tobacco warehouseman, were still sleepy but woke up in time to hear the guards take Scott on his "last mile" walk.

Scott was twice sentenced to death for the September 14, 1945, fatal shooting of Walter Evans, a Greeleyville night policeman.

Death in Four Minutes

The prison's executioner, Sam Cannon, state electrician, applied 2,300 volts for five seconds as the first charge.

Scott gripped the chair convulsively, his right thumb and two adjoining fingers bent grotesquely.

Two other charges followed in quick succession, 1,400 volts and the final 600 volts.

Death was pronounced by Dr. M. Whitfield Cheatham, prison physician, at 7:09 a. m., four minutes and 12 seconds after Scott took his place in the chair.

Scott was married and his wife was said to live in Richmond, Virginia. Prior to the execution, she advised the prison authorities that the family would not claim the body. Scott's parents resided about five miles out of Greeleyville, and his father visited him in the death house. Even so, the parents did not claim the remains of their executed son, the newspaper reported.

Lewis Scott became the two hundred and seventy-third person put to death in South Carolina's electric chair. And he was buried in a prison-made pine board coffin among the unclaimed bodies, in an unmarked grave in the prison cemetery known as Tickleberry.

Fortunately for Roy Singletary, at a death house news event the day before he was to be executed, Rose Marie Stinette testified that he was not involved in the murder of her husband. And, her revealing testimony prompted Gov. Ransome J. Williams to commute Singletary's sentence to life in prison and spare him the torment of taking his seat in the chair.

Chapter 18
Muscleman Cleve Covington

The twenty-six-year-old laborer, Cleve Covington, stood several inches over six feet tall and was said to be as hard as steel. His enormously powerful body, weighing one hundred and ninety-five pounds seemed to have been cast from solid bronze. And the brown-skinned muscles that rippled beneath his clothing could be intimidating. Covington had a normal fear of dying. However, he was terrified at the thought of the high voltage electrical current that would surge through his rock solid body to bring on his death.

Covington received the capital sentence for the bludgeoning death of a man in the small city of Mullins. He told that he and two men had gone upstairs in a tobacco warehouse to talk and that they began drinking. An argument erupted and Watt Martin, a tobacco man down from North Carolina suddenly punched him. Covington told that he picked up a heavy stick lying nearby and used it as a weapon to beat to death the man who struck him.

Covington would have been a formidable adversary even had both men chosen to engage him. However, instead of using his great strength to subdue his antagonist, his drunken anger caused him to grasp the heavy stick and use it as a deadly weapon against Watt Martin.

Under present day conditions, Covington's undue use of force would perhaps be labeled self-defense and he would likely be tried on a lesser charge. Unfortunately for Cleve Covington, he was born fifty years too soon.

That hot summer day, August 23, 1945, turned out to be an ill-fated day for both Covington and the tobacco man, Watt Martin. They went upstairs to talk, take a drink and escape the hubbub of the tobacco auction in the warehouse below, a harmless act that turned out to be tragic for both men.

Covington fled the scene to an unknown destination. Following several months of searching he was located and arrested in one of the big U. S. cities in the northeast. Cleve was aware that he had committed an unpardonable sin with the slaying of a white man, and he fought extradition to South Carolina. However, he was returned to Marion County to be charged with and tried for the slaying of Watt Martin in the small city of Mullins.

He was tried hurriedly and following a short period of deliberations an all-white jury returned its verdict of guilty without a recommendation for mercy. Then on May 10, 1946, Circuit Judge J. L. Lide set June 21 of that year as the date for Cleve Covington to be electrocuted. The sentence was appealed and immediately stayed until the case could be heard by the South Carolina Supreme Court. The high court upheld the lower court's decision and Cleve Covington was resentenced to die on January 3, 1947.

Covington Is Transferred to the Penitentiary

ON THE MORNING OF December 17, 1946 Marion County Sheriff Leon Gasque and his deputies went to shackle the inmate and transfer him to the state penitentiary in Columbia for his execution in early January, 1947. Covington, however, had no intention of going quietly.

As the officers went to fetter him for his trip to the death house, he fought furiously and Sheriff Gasque received a nasty cut on his hand during the melee. Covington's fear induced resistance was not directed at the sheriff or his officers, his determined struggle was to avoid dying in the electric chair. He had no fear of bullets or of being beaten to death in a drunken brawl his horrendous fear was of the electrical current that would course through his body. He begged the sheriff to shoot him as he struggled not to leave his cell. Using tear gas, the deputies were finally able to overcome his great strength and get him into the car for his trip to the state penitentiary in Columbia.

Once at the prison, he was taken directly to the death house. Already held in the death house were the previously mentioned Lewis Scott, Rose Marie Stinette and Roy Singletary.

Everything went well until January 2, the day before Covington was to be executed. On that Thursday morning, my father went to pay the first of his twice daily visits to the doomed inmates. However, he was informed by Sergeant C. Wardlaw Mormon that he could not visit the death house for at least several hours. Dad returned home and even though he knew nothing of the problem at the prison, he knew instinctively that Covington was involved.

My father did not think of Covington as malicious. He was not a street bully he was a polite, warehouse laborer where strength was an asset. He had told my father of his fear of electrocution and Dad felt that he just might lash out when they came to shave his head, in an attempt to force the guards to kill him. As things turned out, my father was discerning in his belief that Covington was involved. However, Dad had no idea that Covington would saw through and bend the iron bars to his cell in a desperate attempt to elude sitting in the chair.

Cleve Covington Escapes from His Cell

THE *COLUMBIA RECORD* GAVE a detailed account of the execution and of the attempted escape in their afternoon edition on January 3, 1947. Following are excerpts from the article by reporter Mark

Warren. The sub headline read, *Prisoner Bends Bars Apart in Death Cell. Powerful Convict Breaks through Two Doors in Escape*

The article continues:

> Despite the fact that he had escaped from his death house cell into the "bull pen" of his final prison home only 24 hours before his execution at 7:04 A.M. today, Cleve Covington, 26-year-old laborer, still had several more barriers to cross before he would have been in the main prison yard. His escape from the death cell, managed by filing a heavy cell bar with a saw he had concealed in his shoe since he was brought here from Marion County jail, December 17th, was said to be the first of its kind since the death house was erected in 1912.

Bends Bar

> After sawing through the bar, Covington, a six foot, two inch, 195 pounder, strictly muscle, no fat, exercised enormous strength to bend the bar and force his body though the hole.

> He then prepared to work on the second of the doors barring his way, but said he used his foot and forced it open. It is a wire screen type door before the barred cell itself. Once outside both barriers, he was free to roam the death house where two other prisoners were behind bars, including Rose Marie Stinette, 41, and Roy Singletary, 22, both of Lake City, who yesterday won a week's reprieve from death sentence for murder.

Stopped In "Bull Pen"

However, Covington was unable to get his freedom beyond the "bull pen" although he did wander into the next door room where the electric chair is located and where he died today. Had he even managed to escape the death house, he would still have faced the problem of escaping from the main prison yard itself. A. Roy Ashley, prison superintendent, said that the death house guard caught Covington outside his cell and placed him in another cell, cell No. 4, within the death house, from which he was led heavily guarded to the chair today.

My father and Chaplin Lester Davis visited with Covington for more than an hour on the morning he was put to death. He was calm and in a reflective mood as his final minutes ticked away, even as the guards and prison officials prepared for his execution. Inmates were usually not shackled as they walked from their cells to the death chamber. However, due to Covington's past behavior, two burly guards were assigned to hold his arms and walk him from his cell to the chair.

Earlier that morning, Covington asked my father to read the prayer from the Bible that "tells about the still waters," and Dad read him the 23rd Psalm. He then began to leaf through his Bible, but could not find the passage he was seeking. The report stated that he exclaimed:

"I do not have time to find it." My father spoke up and said, "That's all right. I will read this one." My father then read some comforting verses from Romans 12. Covington told the three ministers: "I told the Lord about this sin and my other sins.

I'm asking for mercy." Covington continued the conversation by stating, "Yes, I'm guilty!"

He related how that he, another white man, and Watt Martin had gone to a room upstairs in the warehouse at the time of the murder. He told that all three were drinking and that they had gotten into an argument. "I picked up a heavy stick and killed him. He struck me first, though, and then I hit him. We were both fighting."

As Covington sat strapped in the chair and was asked by prison guard captain, Claude A. Sullivan, if he had anything to say, Covington responded, "I speak to all: I ask God to be with me." On further questioning concerning how he had gotten the saw blade, he stated that he had concealed it in his shoe even before he was brought over from the jail in Marion and that no one had helped him get it. He then revealed that he had given it to the other man in the back cell. That, of course, was Roy Singletary.

Shortly after those words, executioner Sam Cannon heard the captain's cane tap the concrete floor, which was his signal to throw the switch. The usual three shocks of twenty-three hundred, fourteen hundred, and five hundred volts of the deadly current were sent surging through the well-muscled body. But due to his size and strength, Dr. M. Whitfield Cheatham stated that his heart continued to beat strongly and that it was necessary to apply another jolt from the high voltage current. He was given two additional shocks of five hundred volts before his heart ceased to function.

Cannon stated that he normally used nine amperes for executions but that he had used eleven amperes on Covington and that, even then, it had taken a bit longer than usual for Covington to die.

Covington was survived by his mother but it is not certain that she claimed his body. Without someone claiming the remains, he would have been buried in an unmarked grave in the prison cemetery, "Tickleberry."

Chapter 19
Rose Marie Stinette

The execution of Rose Marie Stinette was unusual in many ways and the sub-headline in the *Columbia Record*, dated January 17, 1947, stated "Sparks Illuminate Execution in Dark." That headline reflected the uncommon circumstances that transpired during Stinette's stay in the death house. Those words illustrated the conditions that accompanied the execution of Rose Marie whose always cheerful personality had brightened the gloom of the death house for several of her fellow inmates.

Stinette was the first black woman ever to die in the state's electric chair and her execution followed that of a white schoolteacher, Sue Logue, by exactly four years to the day. Logue had the fateful distinction of being the first person of her gender ever electrocuted in South Carolina, and her execution also produced some oddities. However, some of the strangest death house incidents involved the execution of Rose Marie Stinette.

Excerpts from the article written by Mark Warren stated that:

> With a broad smile on her face, short, chunky Rose Marie Stinette, 40-year-old mother of 11 children, stepped into the execution room at the state prison death house this morning, and said, "Good morning, Folks; how is everybody?"

A few minutes later, she was strapped in the electric chair, and three minutes and 40 seconds later was pronounced dead, to pay for a crime she vowed she did not commit.

For the first time in history, too, today's execution was conducted in the dark, for as Sam Cannon, state electrician and official executioner, pulled the switch, the light fuse blew out, plunging the death room into darkness.

Only the light from the electric sparks set off by the current on the woman's arms and head provided an eerie glow to light up the scene like a torch in the night.

Someone struck a match, and as another shot of current was applied, the woman's body seemed almost to leap, tugging at the powerful straps holding her to the chair.

Today in her cell and later in making her deathbed statement, she denied that she bludgeoned her husband, Charles Stinette, a Lake City sawmill worker, to death.

She said, "The man who killed him is on the chain gang. It was Foster Sparkman."

Regarding Roy Singletary, 21, of Lake City, who yesterday won a life commutation from death sentence, she said in her cell in the presence of witnesses: "I'm glad I told the truth about him: he (Roy) wasn't guilty. He didn't do it."

It was also revealed that only one of her eleven children, a married daughter, Katie, still survived. Katie was twenty-two and herself the mother of a five-year-old daughter. However, neither Katie nor her child ever visited Stinette in the death house. Katie told her mother that to visit her in the death house was simply too painful. Stinette never revealed the causes for the deaths of her ten children. However, early and tragic death seemed to be a common thread in the sad story of Rose Marie Stinette.

At the time of her husband's murder, Stinette was allegedly having an affair. And just six months prior to his slaying, an attempt had been made on his life. Four people, including Stinette, were tried for the murder of her spouse, Charles Stinette. And two of the accused men, Foster Sparkman and Sam Frazier, were found guilty and each sentenced to a term of life in prison. Roy Singletary and Rose Marie were also found guilty but, unlike their co-defendants, they each received a sentence of death.

Stinette's testimony helped save Roy Singletary only hours before he was to have died on the same morning with her. However, just days before yielding the state's highest office to Governor-elect Strom Thurmond, Governor Ransome J. Williams granted mercy to Singletary. The commutation was based on Stinette's statements in addition to the changed sentiments of the eleven jurors who had convicted all four defendants. In fact, when announcing his decision to spare Singletary, Governor Williams had made the statement: "I'd rather commute ten guilty ones to life imprisonment than let one innocent person die."

Even though Stinette denied guilt, it is obvious from her testimony that she had an insider's knowledge of the murder of her husband.

Rose Marie was an unusual personality and many of her traits were admirable. Among her more worthy qualities were a cheerful disposition and a positive outlook on life. My father told that even during the final minutes preceding her execution, this one hundred and eighty pound woman, who stood only five feet in height, was going about the business of encouraging others to be positive. He sometimes used Stinette in his sermons to illustrate the comfort that comes to those who believe in Jesus.

Rose Marie's faith is shown in other excerpts taken from the article. These comments were made to the chaplains and other visitors during her final hour as she awaited execution: "Feel so good; I never felt so good a day in my life. I ain't afraid," and "I'm going where there ain't no worry…No aches…no pains."

The newspaper reported: "Present with her in her last hour were the Rev. C. M. (Red) Kelly, prison chaplain; the Rev. Monroe Smith, who has long operated a mission here; the Rev. Edward A. Davis, prison chaplain; the Rev. S. M. Hightower, pastor of the Bethlehem Baptist Church of College Place and St. Mark's of Simpson; and C. H. Simon of 1208 Barnwell Street, a porter and, for four years, a Baptist minister formerly in Georgetown."

All had come to comfort Stinette during her hours of anguish, but, instead of them reassuring her, the doomed woman's strong faith inspired and reassured them.

Stinette told that she and her spouse were childhood neighbors and that they had grown up only doors apart in the same neighborhood and that she had been married when she was only fifteen. And she revealed that, had they lived, they would have celebrated their twenty-fifth anniversary in January, the month of her execution.

She was unschooled and could neither read nor write, so there was no Bible in her cell to provide solace. Instead, she would ask the ministers to read passages from the Bible. My father read from the 53rd and 55th Chapters of Isaiah, and as he read from those scriptures, she suddenly interrupted the reading: "I didn't kill my husband. It happened just like I said. Someone hit me. I'm telling the truth. … On my deathbed, I'm telling the truth."

Moments later, she would repeat those same words in response to Captain Sullivan of the prison guards who came to her cell, looked at her and said, "You know you killed him."

Another time during the morning, she turned to the Reverend Davis and said, "The boy who was supposed to go ... I really cleared him ... because he wasn't the one."

Following the Reverend Smith reading the 23rd and 27th Psalms, which she seemed to like, Stinette commented: "I never had a chance. I would like to live the life of God; I am ready to go."

She went to the chair bubbling with faith and happiness. However, several times during those final hours, she asked if someone could get the governor to commute her sentence to life.

It was reported that once during the morning she began to sway in her cell and broke into a chant of her own composition. The words were:

> "Dear child don't you cry,
> My time's done come.
> Dear brother don't you cry.
> I got to go to meet my Jesus,
> My time's done come."

As she awaited execution, her low, melodious voice could be heard throughout the death house and in other nearby areas of the prison. One veteran guard even commented that he had never experienced such a doomed inmate as Stinette; nor did he ever expect to see another like her.

Dr. M. Whitfield Cheatham, the prison physician, came into the death house some minutes before the execution. Upon seeing him, Stinette called out, "Good morning, Doctor." He asked, "Did you have a good sleep?" She responded: "I had a fine sleep." He continued, "How did you like the fish?" She replied, "It was good." Stinette had requested for her final meal some fish from the low country waters near Greeleyville in Williamsburg County, the area where she was born. And her request for the low country fish, which she had seemed to enjoy, had been granted.

Just before the guards came to escort her to the chair, Stinette, whose head had been shaved and while dressed in the white blouse and khaki pants she would wear into the death chamber, turned to Davis and asked, "Are you coming to my funeral?" He affirmed that not only would he be coming to the funeral but that he would be conducting it for her. My father also participated in the final rites for the happy woman who bravely went to her death just an hour before she was buried.

Some fifty-five individuals came to witness the execution of Stinette. Included among them were several white women, including one white female who had been coming to several of the recent executions.

Due to the blown fuse that had knocked out the lights in the death house, the exhaust fan over the chair failed to function and it was reported that the smell of burning flesh was quite strong.

The body was not claimed by her daughter, Katie, and Stinette went to be interred in the nameless prison cemetery that is known to guards and inmates as "Tickleberry."

Chapter 20
Robert Jordan

The story of Robert Jordan, a twenty-one-year-old black youth from a rural crossroads community near the small city of Florence, is a sad narrative of shock and disbelief on the part of his murder victim, Mrs. S. J. Matthews. Mr. and Mrs. Sam Matthews owned a small general store that was located some fifty yards from their home. Both the home and the store were located on the Matthews farm where Jordan and his family had also resided for almost twenty years, seemingly as sharecroppers. Jordan was married but without children, and he had grown up on the Matthews property. He had been treated as a friend and even somewhat as a member of the extended Matthews family. In fact, on the morning of his execution, he would himself state that he had been practically raised by Mr. and Mrs. Matthews.

Based on what is known of the cordial relationship between the Jordan and Matthews families, it seems that, as was the situation between many black and white individuals during that era of racial segregation, the Matthews and Jordan households enjoyed a mutual bond of respect and trust. Even though ethnically different individuals could not socialize or attend the same public schools together, principled men and women of both races often did form satisfying friendships that were based on fairness, respect, and trust.

Young Robert Jordan, however, would shatter that appreciated relationship between the Jordan and Matthews families when, by his own last hour admission, he had once previously broken into the Matthews home and stolen a pistol. Another prior incident, which he denied to the very end, was when an unknown someone had invaded the Matthews residence and pilfered a goodly sum of cash.

On the morning of his execution, Jordan acknowledged that he failed to consider the consequences when he broke into the home of the property owners where his family lived. He never thought that his ill-considered behavior would lead to the murder of Irene Matthews and to his own execution. The bond that was shattered by his violation of the neighboring residence brought not only death to him and his innocent victim; it also produced untold years of suffering for two hard working and law abiding families.

Home Invaded, Irene Matthews Stabbed

JORDAN ADMITTED THAT HE had seen Irene Matthews leave the house for what he assumed was a visit to the nearby family owned store. And he reasoned that she would be absent for a sufficiently long enough time for him to enter the home and search for the money he intended to steal. However, Matthews was wrapping Christmas presents on that cold December afternoon and she had merely gone out to bring in additional coal for the fireplace.

Jordan told that he had gotten into the house through a dining room window and Mrs. Matthews had caught him inside the kitchen when she re-entered through that entrance with the bucket of coal that she had brought in from the yard. She had seen him instantly and had reactively called out his name in shock and disbelief. He then panicked and began stabbing her with a large case knife. She fought back frantically and was stabbed multiple times as they struggled back and forth throughout the residence. Jordan stated further that she never said anything to him except to call out his name: "Robert!"

Obviously, she could not believe that she was being stabbed by the young man who had grown up on her family's farm, a lad whom she had always treated with kindness and consideration.

After killing Matthews and placing the murder weapon in her lifeless hand, Jordan told that: "He returned to his home and went to bed and that he was asleep when several police officers from Florence arrived and arrested him as a suspect. He related that the officers hit him on the head and that the knots were from the punishing blows," according to the *Columbia Record*.

The Trial and Sentencing

FOLLOWING THE BRUTAL MURDER of the woman who was, in many ways, a surrogate mother to him, Jordan was convicted and sentenced to death following a one-day trial on January 9, 1947, just three weeks following the slaying. Judge W. H. Grimball then set the date of execution to be February 14, 1947.

His lawyers filed no appeal and did nothing to slow the wheels of justice from spinning forth to the inevitable conclusion. And on the morning of February 14, 1947, St. Valentine's Day, Jordan took the walk from his cell into the execution chamber to become the 279th victim of South Carolina's deadly chair.

Several times it has been noted that justice came swiftly during the 1940s. However, the time lapse of less than two full months, just fifty-seven days in the case of Robert Jordan, from the commission of his crime on December 19 to his execution on February 14 of the following year, was seemingly the shortest elapsed time of any capital case during that era. Vigilante justice was not the practice during those decades, but justice was indeed swift, especially so for Robert Jordan who, by his own admission, was guilty of robbery and murder.

Excerpts from Reports of the Execution

FOLLOWING ARE EXCERPTS FROM the *Columbia Record*'s report of the execution dated Feb. 14, 1947:

> Robert Jordan, 21, of Florence, died quietly at 7 a. m. today in the electric chair at the state prison after saying, "I killed her," referring to Mrs. Sam J. Matthews of near Florence, who was stabbed to death in her home, five miles from Florence, December 19. "I want to tell Mr. Matthews I am sorry," Jordan told the prison chaplains who visited him earlier in his cell.

> Jordan said at his trial that he tried to place the blame on Mr. Matthews. "That was a lie. He didn't have anything to do with it. I am guilty. I just said that to help save me."

> Among the sixty spectators present to witness the execution were the prison chaplains, the Reverends C. M. Kelly and E. A. Davis.

> Mr. Sam Matthews, husband of the victim was also present as were Irene Matthews' brother and two brothers-in-law. All had driven over from Florence to witness the execution of the young man who had taken the life of the woman who was so dear to each of them in different ways.

> The relatives stood near Mr. Matthews who was at the right side of the chair watching the proceedings. However, Mr. Matthews was heard to say, "I'm not nervous" as they watched his reaction.

He was seen to nod his head when he heard that Jordan had expressed his sorrow for the killing.

It was not until today that Jordan made the full confession. Up until this time he had protested his innocence.

Captain R. Fuller Goodman of the prison official staff was in charge of today's execution.

After Jordan was strapped in the chair, Goodman asked Jordan if he had anything to say.

It was then that Jordan repeated the confession that he had made several times earlier in his cell.

He asked that the Bible be read and the Rev. Kelly asked the Rev. Davis to give a quotation, the latter selecting the 27th Psalm which he intoned in a deep voice and with feeling.

The mask was then applied after Jordan told Dr. M. Whitfield Cheatham, prison physician, that he had no other requests.

Switch Is Pulled

Sam Cannon, state electrician, pulled the switch and Jordan gripped the chair convulsively.

The execution required 4:48.5 minutes—longer than normal—and began with 2300 volts at nine amperes for five seconds, stepped down to 1400, then 500 and for a minute back up the scale as the first charges failed to bring immediate death.

The report stated that several women were present and that their faces reflected the strain. However, none had fainted, as had several female witnesses to past executions. It is noteworthy that several men also fainted at the sight and stench of an electrocution. A Nazarene pastor who was a close friend of my father was one such individual. Dad's clergy colleague had quite suddenly fainted and collapsed to the concrete floor as he witnessed an execution.

The Parental Anguish

ROBERT JORDAN'S HEARTBROKEN RELATIVES visited the death house during his final days of confinement, and he expressed his anxiety over the disposition of his body to his wife and parents. They assured him that his body would be returned home for a memorial service and buried in ground that was familiar to him. And they kept that promise.

Chapter 21
Talmadge Haggins

T almadge Haggins, a twenty-five-year-old black man, died in the electric chair on April 18, 1947. His was the first in a trio of executions that year for the unrelated killings of cabdrivers near the upstate cities of Chester and Lancaster. The separate cases, though in no way connected, had interesting similarities. In addition to Haggins, the two black men put to death for slaying a cabdriver near one of those small cities was Leonard Pringle and Ernest Willis, the subjects in another chapter.

Haggins was executed for the senseless killing of Oscar Benjamin Powers, a twenty-three-year-old cabbie who was white. Powers was shot through the head and robbed on September 19, 1946. Following an intensive police investigation, the trail led eventually to Haggins who was not directly but circumstantially linked to the slaying. Details of the Powers murder are sketchy and a search through various archives revealed nothing to irrefutably connect or clear Haggins of the crime. However, from the moment of his arrest until he took his seat in the chair, Haggins denied his guilt.

A measure of irony is manifest in the unrelated murders and the subsequent executions of the three young men; namely that none of the trio was from South Carolina. Pringle and Willis were from Brooklyn, New York, and Haggins from Baltimore. All

155

were in South Carolina to visit relatives or work as laborers in the Lancaster-Chester area.

Following his conviction, the death sentence was passed by Judge J. F. Eatmon at the conclusion of the short trial on February 26, 1947. Even though it took a while longer than was normally required to connect a suspect to the crime, from the time of the cabdriver's murder until Haggins was tried and convicted had taken but five months.

He was taken directly from the county jail to his cell in the death house, where he spent the final eighteen days of his young life. The case drew minimal publicity, and my father was unaware of Haggins until he was placed in his cell in the death house. Even though my father visited him daily as he awaited the executioner, the chaplain learned almost nothing of Haggins' background or about his family prior to him being convicted for the murder of the young cabdriver, Benjamin Powers.

The *Columbia Record* reported the execution in their edition dated April 18, 1947. Reporter Arthur Keeney wrote:

> Haggins entered the death chamber at 7:04 a. m. singing a Negro spiritual, possibly inspired by the hymnal which was left in his cell, the cover of which bore the words, "Lord open Thou my lips and my mouth shall show forth Thy praise." He was strapped securely into the chair and asked if he had anything to say. He responded: "I wish somebody would tell the boy's mother that I didn't do the crime. I wish somebody would ask her to bless me like I asked my mother to bless her boy. And I want to thank the governor for all he did for me."

The report told that Haggins seemed concerned over the disposition of his remains. He wanted his body returned to Baltimore and not buried in an unmarked grave in the prison cemetery. Haggins was said to have asked Captain R. Fuller

Goodman as he was being strapped into the chair, and just before uttering his final words to the victim's mother, "Is Undertaker Robinson here?"

Haggins had given his religion as Methodist. Nonetheless, he was holding a Roman Catholic crucifix in his left hand when he took his seat in the chair in which he was about to die. The symbolic object was removed just seconds before twenty-three hundred volts of current was sent surging into his youthful body. Some three and a half minutes following the first jolt of high voltage current, the fifty individuals who were there to witness the death of their fellow human being would hear Dr. M. W. Cheatham, the prison physician pronounce him dead.

Talmadge Haggins, the young man who denied his guilt right up until his final moment, had just become the 282nd person to die in South Carolina's electric chair, some seven months following the murder for which he was convicted. The strong young man from Baltimore would be returned to his home in a coffin. However, even though Haggins was married, it was his mother who claimed the body for burial.

The news article told that he left behind in his cell some notes, a hymnal, a Bible, four slices of bread and an empty cigarette package. Except for the Bible and the hymnal which were left in place, the other items were removed by death house guards.

It was also reported that: "Haggins left one dollar each for two other Negroes condemned to die within the next two weeks, Freddie Jones and Roosevelt Miller. The money was delivered to them by Captain Goodman." Such small sums were typically used by condemned inmates to have guards buy them things like cigarettes, candy, and soda from the canteen at the prison.

My father, the sincere and kindly man who people instinctively trusted, and for whom they would pour out their innermost feelings as was done by inmates awaiting execution in other cases, was never able to form such a bond with Haggins. Even though Haggins entered the execution chamber singing a Negro spiritual and holding a crucifix, it seems that he never once professed a personal relationship with the Almighty to either of the chaplains.

My father never felt fully convinced that Haggins was guilty of the shooting of the cabdriver, and Haggins was reluctant to talk much with him. However, neither did Dad feel that Haggins was totally without knowledge of the events that transpired before the stiffened body of Benjamin Powers was found along a remote stretch of the highway between Lancaster and Great Falls on the morning of September 20, 1946.

Powers had been shot through the head, and his pockets turned inside out when his remains were discovered just hours following his slaying and shortly before his stolen taxi turned up abandoned in the city of Columbia. Haggins was somehow connected to the stolen vehicle by the investigating authorities but it was not clear as to just how he became the suspect.

Dad always hoped against hope that the State of South Carolina had not executed an innocent Talmadge Haggins for a murder he did not commit. It should be noted, however, that condemned criminals sometimes use their own self-serving interpretations of the law as justification for denying their guilt. Examples of such reasoning are illustrated in the chapters on Sammie Osborne and Charles Gilstrap.

There is no awareness of such reasoning by Haggins to justify denial of the crime for which he was put to death. Haggins steadfastly denied having knowledge of the murder of Powers, even though circumstantial evidence connected him to the stolen cab that was found in Columbia shortly after the murder.

Chapter 22
Freddie Jones

Freddie Jones, a nineteen-year-old black youth and a veteran of World War II took his seat in the electric chair on April 25, 1947, for the capital offense of murder. Jones was convicted and sentenced to die for the stabbing death of a young Chester County woman, Gladys Smith Woods, in the spring of 1946 when he attempted to rob her. He admitted guilt during questioning, an acceptance of blame that he never retracted, and his guilt was not an issue.

Jones was tried just weeks after the murder, and on March 8, 1946, following a very brief trial and short period of deliberation, the jurors returned their verdict of guilty without a recommendation of mercy. Immediately following the verdict, Judge G. Duncan Bellinger sentenced Jones to be executed on April 18, 1946, a time period of less than six weeks following his conviction.

Jones' court-appointed attorney stated his intent to appeal the sentence, a procedure that stayed the death penalty until the appeal was heard, and a decision rendered by the South Carolina Supreme Court. However, the attorney failed to serve notice of the appeal until April 6, which was almost a month after Jones had been sentenced and only twelve days before he was scheduled to die. In fact, he had already been transferred to the death house and was being held there when notice of the appeal became known to the solicitor.

Some four days following the prosecutor receiving notice of the attorney's intent to appeal, Jones was removed from the death house on April 10 and added to the "Yard Count of Colored Males" at the main penitentiary. He would then be held in the maximum security section of the prison that was designated Cell Block F to await the outcome of his appeal, a futile action that would delay his execution by just over a year.

Governor Ransome J. Williams

GOV. RANSOME J. WILLIAMS, upon learning the execution date had been stayed by the South Carolina Supreme Court, ordered the inmate be moved from the prison and taken to the state hospital to be examined for his mental condition. However, for reasons that were not learned during our research of the archived records, Jones was never transferred to the psychiatric institution. Instead, he was examined by competent psychiatrists while in his cell on death row before it was determined he was sane.

Governor J. Strom Thurmond

THE APPEAL LAY DORMANT at the state Supreme Court until that panel heard the appeal some weeks after Williams left office in January of 1947. Williams lost his re-election bid to political newcomer, Judge J. Strom Thurmond the previous November, and the high court did not hear the Jones appeal until weeks after Thurmond was sworn in as governor.

On March 4, 1947, Judge J. Frank Eatmon of the South Carolina Supreme Court dismissed the appeal on behalf of Freddie Jones. Jones was then taken immediately from the state prison and returned to the Chester County Court House for resentencing. That same afternoon Jones again stood before a judge at the bar of justice to learn that he would die in the chair at the state penitentiary on April 25, 1947. Following his resentencing, Jones was returned to the penitentiary and placed again in Cell Block F to await transfer to the death house and his date with the executioner.

My father and Chaplain E. A. "Lester" Davis visited him frequently during the year he awaited execution. Dad described Jones as a sullen individual who never denied his guilt or expressed remorse for the slaying of Gladys Wood. Jones related that he was married and had grown up as a farmer in North Carolina, but he seemingly had little contact with his family.

Freddy Jones was said to be of average height and weight and from all outward appearances he seemed benign and harmless. However, the real Jones was a vicious young man who had slain an innocent young woman while attempting to rob her. In his efforts to prevent Gladys Woods from being identified, the taciturn Jones had mutilated her physical features by brutally cutting the skin from her face. Jones never denied the alleged brutality and he voluntarily admitted to having committed the unprovoked murder of the hapless young woman.

The Final Days and the Execution

TWENTY DAYS BEFORE HIS execution, Jones was again moved from his death row cell and back to one of the six small cells in the death house. There he would await his appointment to be strapped into the lethal chair and render his life for the heartless murder of an innocent woman.

Governor Thurmond announced several days preceding the execution that he would not intervene to prevent the sentence from being carried out. With that declaration by the governor the fate of the young World War II veteran, Freddie Jones was sealed.

The execution was reported in the *Columbia Record* edition of April 25, 1947, following the execution that morning. The report read:

> Freddie Jones, a 19-year-old veteran of WW II, died quietly today in the electric chair at the death house at the state's prison, for the mutilation death last spring of Gladys Smith Woods of Chester County.
>
> Jones, who admitted the stabbing death of the young Chester County woman, had no comment to make today as he was led to the chair.
>
> Capt. R. Fuller Goodman was in charge of the execution, and Jones was apparently calm as he entered the death chamber.

The article was not typical of the coverage usually devoted to executions by that publication. Notwithstanding the brutality of the crime, and that the Jones execution was deserving of considerable print coverage, the report of the Jones execution was moved from the usual Page 1 location all the way back to Page 6A.

Chapter 23
John Dickerson

John Dickerson, a thirty-five-year-old black man from the small city of Manning went to his death in the electric chair on the morning of May 2, 1947. He was executed for the murder of twenty-four-year-old Louise Stevens, a young woman with whom he was acquainted and with whom he had argued over things that were unspecified.

Dickerson denied the murder of the young black woman until only minutes before he was executed. However, the anxious Dickerson, who was described by the *Columbia Record*'s Mark Warren as "pacing his cell like a caged tiger" on the morning he was put to death, felt the need to come clean during his final hour. It was in his death cell and only minutes before his execution when Dickerson finally admitted to cutting to death his young female acquaintance. The murder occurred in a sandpit near Charleston where the two had been "drinking and fussing," according to Dickerson.

The afternoon edition of the *Columbia Record* covered the execution at the prison that morning. Excerpts from the article are as follows:

> "The last man who died told me he owed his downfall to marijuana cigarettes," the Rev. C.

M. (Red) Kelly, prison chaplain and pastor of the Nazarene church here, told Dickerson.

The Rev Mr. Kelly read some comforting verses from the Bible, as Dickerson continued to pace his cell while chain-smoking cigarettes.

"He has placed his trust in the Lord," the Rev. Edward A. Davis, prison chaplain and pastor of the Bethlehem Baptist Church, said of Dickerson. "He is standing by me," Dickerson added.

Dickerson said he had not seen his wife, Alma A. Dickerson of Manning, or his three children, since he entered the state's penitentiary.

Among the fifty-five spectators who came to witness the death of John Dickerson were several ministers. Included among them was H.D. "Bubby" Davis, a Nazarene song evangelist from Langley, one of the "Horse Creek" valley towns near Aiken, South Carolina.

Singing in the Death House

MY FATHER OFTEN ASKED Bubby Davis, his friend and colleague, to come and visit the death house where Davis would sing and play the guitar for the men who were facing execution. The song evangelist was happy to comply with Dad's requests for those death cell rendezvous where his playing and singing meant so much to those individuals who faced death with but little hope.

Quite frequently doomed inmates requested a favorite song or hymn, and seldom was Davis unable to accommodate them. At times, Davis and a condemned convict would blend their voices in harmony and the death house would reverberate with the words and tunes of old hymns, pop songs and Negro spirituals.

Among the appreciative listeners were my father and the guards who were filling death house duties. Chaplain E. A. Davis, the little black minister with a giant-sized personality and a deep singing voice, would sometimes blend his rich baritone with the voices of the guitar strumming Bubby Davis and the doomed inmate.

The visits by the song evangelist were enjoyable and comforting for the men facing execution. They would frequently ask if he would come and sing again before they were put to death. And when it was possible, Davis went an additional time to provide an hour or two of guitar music and singing for the condemned prisoners.

John Dickerson was one of those for whom Bubby Davis sang a death house concert. And while no one could placate the men who so violated the dictates of society, my father felt that by having them listen to the old hymns and spirituals, that they were somehow comforted. Davis sometimes sang during Sunday morning services at the prison chapel. And when he sang, many inmates who did not usually attend worship services would come to hear him pick his guitar and croon the sacred old hymns of the church.

The Execution

DICKERSON MADE NO FINAL statement when asked by guard Captain R. Fuller Goodman if he had anything he wanted to say before dying. The captain repeated the question to which he got a second negative response. Goodman then stepped away from the chair and tapped his cane on the floor as the signal for executioner Sam Cannon to throw the switch and end the life of John Dickerson.

The *Columbia Record* report stated that: "The first application sent 2,300 volts of current surging into the body of John Dickerson. The second and third charges, routinely reduced to 1,350 and 600 volts, were then applied. As was typical of those executed, the small-bodied Dickerson succumbed more readily to the deadly current than did most of the larger and stronger individuals who were electrocuted. Dickerson was pronounced dead some three minutes and thirteen seconds after receiving the initial shock."

Dickerson was scheduled to die a month earlier, but Gov. Strom Thurmond had granted a thirty-day stay of execution to study the case. At noon on May 1st, the day before the scheduled execution the next morning, the pardon board announced that it would not act to overturn the sentence. With that announcement, Dickerson's fate was sealed and he died on May 2, 1947.

Dickerson was married and the father of three children. However, they did not visit during his incarceration or claim the body. Thus, John Dickerson, the 281st person executed in the state's electric chair, went to his eternal rest in an unmarked grave in Tickleberry.

Chapter 24
William A. Davis

The execution of rapist William A. Davis on June 20, 1947 was unusual in that Davis, as he sat strapped in the chair, made a plea for "racial amity." The twenty-seven-year-old black male admitted raping a white woman just over two months earlier, on the evening of April 15. And, as he sat in the chair where his deadly punishment was to be inflicted, he turned remorseful and contemplative.

It is noteworthy that during the decade of the 1940s, that it had taken only two months and five days from the date of the rape on April 15, to the day when Davis was put to death on June 20, 1947. Justice did indeed come quickly during that era, especially for those who either raped or committed murder. And the amount of time it took from the date of the crime to the day when Davis was put to death was a typically short two, three or four months during that era.

Davis' violation of the woman happened in the city of Sumter, a small town that was known for its genteel customs and where violent crime was unusual. The city was proud of its namesake, General Thomas Sumter, a Revolutionary War hero who was known as the "Fighting Gamecock." Fort Sumter, from whence the Civil War was ignited, was also named in honor of the celebrated general. The city was proud of its heritage, and violent crime was not tolerated. Those who enacted violence were dealt with swiftly as was the situation with William A. Davis following his breaking into her home and attacking the married woman.

Davis contemptibly violated the mores of that proud little city when earlier on the evening of the assault he had already invaded at least three additional homes in that same immediate area. He was an intelligent young man who seemed obsessed with seeking out trouble on that particular nightfall.

Manhunt Started Immediately

THE PEOPLE OF SUMTER learned of the rape when it was reported the following afternoon, April 16, 1947, in the Sumter *Daily Item*. The sub-headline on page one of the *Daily Item* read, "Manhunt on for Negro Assailant". Excerpts from the article stated:

> City, county and state police are staging an intensive manhunt today for a young negro who, Chief of Police W. C. Kirven said, entered a Sumter home and criminally assaulted the wife of a prominent Sumter man last night at around 7:45.

> Chief Kirven said today that a continuous search was made during the night without results, but that several persons were picked up for questioning.

> Police gave the following description of the negro, adding that he was believed to be a sex maniac: 20 to 25 years of age; 5 feet, 4 inches to 5 feet, 6 inches tall; 135 to 140 pounds in weight; black or dark brown complexion; nappy hair, long face, large eyes, dressed in dark clothes, bareheaded and barefooted when he entered the home and

had a large bandana handkerchief tied around his face.

The negro is said to have entered at least three homes before the attack and one afterwards.

During the search last night in the neighborhood where the attack occurred, a negro who was walking along a street ran into some shrubbery nearby and a shot was fired in that direction, but that person, police said, did not answer to the description of the assailant.

The article also revealed that the City of Sumter and Sumter County were individually offering five hundred dollar rewards, for a total of one thousand dollars, for anyone who could provide information leading to the arrest and conviction of the assailant.

Arrest is Made

THE SUMTER *DAILY ITEM* on April 19 announced the arrest of William Davis with the bold, page one headline: "Negro Attacker Seized, Admits Guilt, Is Carried to Columbia." The sub-headline continued: "Found Hiding in Clarendon at 1:45 A.M." Excerpts from the story stated:

William Davis, young Negro hunted for assaulting a white Sumter woman, and the breaking into of several Sumter homes was captured early this morning about 1:45 by a group of law enforcement officers in a tract of woodland near a relative's home just over the Clarendon County line. The announcement, which came from the office of Sheriff W. J. Seale, said Davis freely admitted his guilt of the crimes with which he was charged and with little questioning by officers.

Davis was carried to the state penitentiary in Columbia for safekeeping immediately after his arrest.

"In some instances, Davis was able to give the street number of residences he entered and in every case he named the street," Sheriff Seale's statement continued.

The sheriff revealed that officers from various city, county, and state jurisdictions worked throughout the entire manhunt with but minimal breaks to rest in their efforts to capture the suspect. He told that systematic searches of buses on the (Manning, Sumter, Florence) road were instituted, but with no results. And he offered particularly high praise for the Columbia Detective Division which was involved. The Columbia detectives had watched constantly for Davis in several locations where he was known to have worked previously in that city.

Additional excerpts from the April 19 announcement of the arrest stated:

The arrest of Davis ended a day and night search since last Tuesday when the crimes were committed.

There had been numerous rumors of the Negro's arrest since Wednesday when it became known that Davis was the main suspect. His whereabouts became definitely known to law enforcement authorities on yesterday afternoon when Policeman Kinney of the city police received a tip that the Negro was hiding near his uncle's home just over the Clarendon County line. Davis was said to be a native of Clarendon County.

Chief W. C. Kirven of the city police and all his officers had been following every lead since the crimes, and the city force, along with the other officers, were breathing easier today—for they had the double duty of searching for the suspect and protecting the city and the county at the same time.

During that era before the Civil Rights movement would end segregation and give the black man his overdue rights as a full-fledged citizen, manhunts by officers from many jurisdictions, including scores of civilian volunteers, were not uncommon. This was especially true when a white woman was violated in a black-on-white crime situation.

It is evident that Davis, in his final statement, is expressing his own recognition that his senseless violation of a white woman had done nothing to help his people's long and rightful struggle for equality.

Race Relations and Civic Pride Reflected in Mayor's Letter

FOLLOWING THE MANHUNT, SUMTER Mayor Edwin B. Boyle, in a letter to the editor of the Sumter *Daily Item*, would say:

Dear Sir:

Through your column, I as Mayor, wish to convey the thanks of all citizens of the city and community, as well as the city officials to all of those who had a part in apprehending and arresting the guilty person who perpetrated Sumter's most fiendish offense.

To the law enforcement officers of the governor's constabulary, directed under Mr. Dollard; to the highway patrol officers under Lieutenant Kinsey; to the county officers under Sheriff Seale; to our own police force under Chief Kirven; and all citizens of both races who assisted and evidenced the earnest desire to apprehend the guilty party, though known to be of their own race.

Such co-operation in time of trouble or emergency is what makes for a better Sumter.

Through the cooperation, diligence and efficiency on the part of all, especially the officers of the law, state, county and city was the right man arrested. A speedy but fair trial is expected.

Respectfully,

Edwin B. Boyle, Mayor, April 22, 1947

The Execution

THE *COLUMBIA RECORD* REPORTED the execution in their afternoon edition dated June 20, 1947. The page two headlines read: "Rapist Dies with Racial Amity Plea." Excerpts from the report by columnist Arthur G Keeney told that:

William A. Davis, convicted of the rape of a prominent Sumter woman in her home on April 15, died in the electric chair at the South Carolina state penitentiary at 7:08 a.m. today. His last words were tantamount to a plea for interracial understanding.

The small, wiry, 27-year-old Negro entered the death chamber at 7:01 a.m. and was strapped in by prison trustees. He showed no sign of emotion.

The presiding official, Capt. R. Fuller Goodman, asked Davis for any final comment.

Plea for His Race

"I want to say, Captain," the Negro began, "that I know your race is a good race. My race is a good race. You folks here may never forgive me for what I done. My folks may never forgive me for bringing shame on them. But I know the good Lord will forgive me."

He then continued with a description of his early life and schooling. "I was brought up in the church," he said. "If I had stayed with my mother I would have been all right. But I started drinking and hiding and running around with a bad crowd and I got in trouble. I know I done wrong. I want the good Lord to forgive me. My race is a good race and I don't want you to hold what I done against them." Turning to prison (Negro) chaplain, the Rev. E. A. Davis, he asked: "Reverend, I wonder if you'd sing that song just once more."

"That's up to the captain," the Rev. Davis said.

Hymn is Sung

Captain Goodman nodded and the small, rotund chaplain began the first verse of "Let the Lower Lights Be Burning." The condemned man joined him and they sang for a few moments.

When they had finished, Goodman ordered the mask and headpiece set in place and, as the trustees complied with his orders, Davis said quietly, "Lord have mercy." As they finished, he added: "Goodbye, everyone."

State Electrician Sam W. Cannon pulled the switch that ended Davis' life. Davis was pronounced dead four minutes and five seconds later.

Throughout these chapters there are similarities in the final requests by those who were executed. In addition to fried chicken being the most requested last meal, many doomed inmates received comfort from the old Christian hymns they remembered from childhood. My father told that a number of the doomed were comforted when they would request, and his associate chaplain, the personable little Reverend E. A. "Lester" Davis, would oblige by using his superb baritone voice to sing the hymns and spirituals that were requested.

Chapter 25
J. C. Sims

J. C. Simms, a thirty-three-year-old black man went to his death in the electric chair on the morning of July 11, 1947, for the murder of Anderson police officer, Ed Sanders. Sanders had surprised Sims back on April 15, while he was in the act of stealing sugar from an Anderson creamery. Sims fired the shots that killed the patrolman when the officer opened the door to enter the storage area where the culprit was about the business of burglary.

Sims claimed not to have known that Sanders was a police officer and that he fired impulsively at the person who had interrupted him in the process of stealing more than five tons of the creamery's sweeteners. Sims never denied the shooting, and he claimed to be rueful over the slaying. Nonetheless, he had gone armed and prepared to shoot if interrupted. And, for so doing, he had no one to blame but himself for the senseless killing that would send him to die in the chair.

It is noteworthy that Sims fought furiously with the policemen who apprehended him. He engaged them in a three-hour shootout before the officers could get him subdued. Official records indicate that Sims was not a stranger to trouble. He had a compound fracture scar, and the scar from a gunshot wound on his left leg when he was booked into the penitentiary.

The Trial and Execution

SIMS WAS TRIED IN one month subsequent to the crime and on May 16, in a one-day trial his jury needed only eleven minutes of deliberations to declare him guilty. Judge G. B. Greene immediately sentenced him to die on July 11. The verdict was not appealed and he died on that date, a date that followed Officer Sanders' murder by only eighty seven days. Justice did indeed come quickly in the 1940s.

The Columbia Record reported the execution in their afternoon edition of July 11, following the execution that morning. The page one sub-headline and excerpts from the article by Reporter Mark Warren are as follows:

"I'm Sorry," Killer Says before Death

J.C. Sims, 33, of Anderson, who died at 7:04 a.m. today in the electric chair at the state prison's death house, told visitors in his cell, "I regret I killed the policeman."

Brought into the execution chamber, Sims shook his head in negative fashion when guard Captain R. Fuller Goodman asked, "J. C., have you any statement you would like to make?"

Then Dr. M. Whitfield Cheatham, prison physician asked, "Nothing to say, J. C.?" He again shook his head.

It was observed that Sims was deep in prayer as guards placed the straps across his body.

Dies Quickly

Captain Goodman gave the tap of the cane on the concrete floor of the death house and Electrician Cannon shoved the switch in place. A yellow flame leaped from the back of Sims' neck and he seemed to collapse instantly.

The voltage was the normal series of 2,300 volts down to 1,350 and then 600. The voltage was again raised to the maximum and bounced for a minute.

Although he was of husky build, he seemed to die quickly as no pulse could be felt after the first voltage was applied.

The execution report stated that there were about forty spectators present for the execution and that several were observed to place handkerchiefs over their nostrils. Among the witnesses were a law enforcement captain and nearly a dozen patrolmen from the Anderson police department.

Also present in the death house were several clergy friends of my father. The visitors included the Reverend J. Raymond Parker of Little Rock, Arkansas, who was conducting revival services at the Reverend M. P. Kolb's pastorate, the Camden Church of the Nazarene. Kolb was also present as were two Catholic priests who came to offer spiritual services to the doomed inmate who was reported to be of that faith.

Baptized Yesterday

ACCORDING TO THE NEWSPAPER article:

"In the death house, Sims was baptized yesterday noon, it was related by the prison chaplain, the Rev. C. M. Kelly, and the Rev. E. A. Davis.

"Both chaplains reported that Sims had readily admitted to his guilt from the start—to which the prisoner added his assent—and the condemned man said, 'I have accepted the Lord.'"

Sims was married and the father of a toddler son. Nonetheless, he failed to fulfill his responsibilities to his wife and child when he attempted to make a quick dollar by stealing eleven thousand pounds of sugar from the creamery. That flawed exercise of judgment led to his own senseless death in the chair in addition to the tragic death of police officer Ed Sanders.

A bit of trivia provided in the newspaper report was that:

'Today's execution was the 42nd witnessed by a Negro death house attendant, Arthur Rush, 28, of Orangeburg. It is Rush's duty to supervise the removal of the dead men. Rush is serving 11 years for the slaying some years ago of a friend during a 'skin game' argument and is scheduled to come up for release October 10."

Buried in Tickleberry

SIMS' BODY WAS NOT claimed and he, the 286th victim of the state's electric chair, suffered the indignity of interment in the prison-owned cemetery Tickleberry.

Trustees, accompanied by guards, loaded the body of Sims aboard a flatbed truck and hauled it to a waiting grave in the cemetery. There, the Rev. E. A. Davis read verses from the scriptures and my father prayed as trustees lowered the pine-board coffin into ground.

Sims' toddler son would never know his father. However, it is hoped that he and other such children were able to overcome the trauma of being the offspring of an executed parent.

Chapter 26
Bert Grant Jr.

The sub-headline on page two of the *Columbia Record*, dated July 25, 1947, stated: "Negro Eats Chicken, Then Dies in Chair."

Bert Grant Jr., an eighteen-year-old black youth from the Hartsville area, had been put to death earlier that morning for the crime of assault with intent to ravish. Grant was convicted of the attack on a young white mother as her small children watched in horror.

The attempted rape had occurred on May 24 and in less than a month following the attack Grant was tried, convicted and sentenced to death on June 19, at the county courthouse in Darlington. Judge J. Woodrow Lewis set the date for Grant's execution to be on July 25, just two months and one day following his mindless crime. His was one of the speediest renderings of justice ever, even for that era.

Grant had invaded the home and was attempting to drag his screaming victim into the yard as her three small children watched terrified as their mother fought her unknown assailant. She kicked, scratched and fought furiously and Grant was scratched heavily before she managed to escape. In fact, a bloody scratch on his face was what helped her to identify him as her assailant when he was apprehended within the hour on a railroad trestle that was only a mile from her home.

Grant was a powerful young man who stood over six feet tall and weighed 182 pounds. He was a laborer in the cotton hauling business, and lifting the heavy bales of cotton had given him a rock solid body. Due to his unusual strength and physical conditioning, the young mother was fortunate to have thwarted his degenerate intent to force himself on her in the presence of her terrified youngsters.

Even though Bert was unable to force penile penetration on the young parent, his failure to do so in no way diminished the seriousness of the charge against him. Conviction on either rape, or assault with intent to ravish was a capital offense and a number of young males were executed on those charges during dads' years as chaplain. The forceful attempt to violate a woman, even when not successful, was simply not tolerated.

The Grant case received minimal publicity and no appeals were filed to delay his date with death.

Bert Grant Jr. Electrocuted

THE COLUMBIA RECORD PUBLISHED an informative account of the crime and Grant's execution on the afternoon of July 25, 1947. Reporter Mark Warren witnessed the execution that morning and the following excerpts are from his contribution:

> His execution was only 15 minutes off but Bert Grant Jr., 18, of Hartsville, commented in his death cell at the state's prison death house, "I think I better eat a little more chicken."

> He had a hearty appetite for chicken for his last supper last night, then had a second plentiful helping, and still had some on a plate in his cell today. "It sure is good," he commented.

Denies Criminal Assault

Young Grant, a Negro youth who could neither read nor write, said in his last statement before he died that he was not guilty of criminal assault. A prison guard commented, however, "The man had never understood that attempted assault also carried the death penalty." He was convicted of the latter charge.

Says Shortened His Days

In his cell, Grant told his last visitors, "I haven't lived half my time. I shortened my days myself."

He asked the Rev. E.A. Davis, a prison chaplain, to write "to my daddy ... Tell him I'm going to Heaven. I have a grandmother up there. She has been dead over five months."

Expresses His Sorrow

"I'm sorry for what I done and I want you all to forgive me," he told the Rev. C. M. Kelly, the Rev. Mr. Davis, and a Benedict College student, the Rev R. C. Wilson of Houston, Texas.

"I hate to go," he continued, "but I got to."

The Rev Mr. Kelly read to Grant from the 46th Psalm. "That's our only trust, in the Lord," he told the condemned youth.

Chaplain Davis read to him the 121st Psalm and also repeated with him the Lord's Prayer.

Praises Prison Guards

"I appreciate to the highest what you all did for me," Grant said to one of the prison guards.

"They (the guards), the captain, the stewards and all the gentlemen were real good to me," Grant said.

He asked the death cell guards to join in prayer for him also. He seemed pleased when one of the guards promised to make a prayer.

"Hello, boys," Grant said to some Negro prison workers who perform duties in the death house. "Well, you see the shape I'm in.

"Trust in God" he admonished them.

"I have prayed to God that the world will live. I'm going to another life. You all will know where to find me. I'm ready to go."

Says To Obey Parents

Grant said he wanted to leave one word to the children of South Carolina: "Obey your parents." He said the trouble began because he failed to do that when he was a child.

Deputy Sheriff Williams said that "Grant had graduated in crime, starting with small thefts such as the theft of a bicycle.

"Later he found a key to a post office box and used it for a series of petty thefts, until apprehended in the act, and for which he drew a sentence to the John J. Richards industrial school in Columbia (Negro state reformatory)."

After that, Deputy Williams said, he drew a North Carolina sentence.

Rather Die Here, Grant Says

Grant said he was happy for one thing: "I'd rather burn here than in the everlasting fire."

"He had several letters and a card in his cell from a Charleston woman who wrote him a number of comforting epistles," the Rev. Mr. Kelly said.

The article goes on to relate that, following the customary three high voltage jolts of electrical current, Grant's heart continued to beat strongly. A second series of shocks was then applied, and Grant succumbed to the deadly current.

Grant left his Bible in the cell for another occupant to read at some time in the future. And he gave his cigarettes and matches to another death house inmate, Willie Pooler, who was confined in a cell on the opposite side of the death house and would die the following Friday.

Chapter 27
Willie Pooler

W illie Pooler was a nineteen-year-old black youth who had acted on spur of the moment impulses to criminally assault a sixty-seven-year-old grandmother, a white woman, a crime for which he took his seat in the electric chair on August 1, 1947. The assault had occurred on May 25 of that same year, and it had taken just two months and one week for the illiterate Willie Pooler to be arrested, charged, tried, and executed.

The woman had been assaulted near a remote stretch of the Timmonsville road, a rural two-lane highway that connected Darlington, the county seat, with the outlying towns and crossroad communities. Before NASCAR came to rev up the economy, a rural area economy that was dependent on cotton and tobacco, violent crime was not a major concern. The high school sports venues, churches, cotton and tobacco warehouses were where people gathered to form the strong bonds that held the isolated communities together.

Nonetheless, despite the illusions of tranquility that prevailed in those towns and crossroads communities, violence was a sinister presence that would occasionally boil to the surface. And the week prior to Willie Pooler taking his seat in the chair, another of the areas native sons, Bert Grant Jr. had succumbed to the deadly current. In addition to Bert Grant and Willie Pooler, seven others from the Sumter, Darlington, Florence, and Manning area were executed during the years my father served as chaplain. Among those put to death were Cleve Covington, William A. Davis, Rose Marie Stinette, Frank Timmons, George Stinney Jr., Robert Jordan, and Wash Pringle. Except for Stinette, each of those nine individuals was put to death for the capital offenses of murder, rape, or assault with intent to ravish.

Willie Pooler Executed

THE COLUMBIA RECORD, DATED August 1, 1947, covered the execution of Willie Pooler on that morning and excerpts from the article by reporter Mark Warren are as follows:

> The first warm rays of the morning sunshine filtered through the barred windows of the state's death house today and gave Willie Pooler, a 19-year-old Darlington County Negro, his last look at nature before his death in the electric chair.
>
> It was a quiet execution and Pooler was pronounced dead by Dr. M. Whitfield Cheatham, prison physician, at 2:29, 1-2 minutes after guards strapped him in the chair.
>
> He said today that he had made his profession of Christian faith, and was baptized last week with another Darlington County youth, Bert Grant Jr., 18, who died last Friday.
>
> He today requested the Negro chaplain, the Rev. E. A. Davis, and the Negro chaplain at the Veterans Hospital, the Rev. G. W. Williams, that a letter be sent to a Darlington friend, William Samuel of Coker Street, "To pray for me." He said

he wanted to testify to Samuel of the Christian way of life. Pooler was calm. He sat in his cell and listened to words of the Bible as read by his visiting ministers.

"When he came here," the Rev. Davis commented, "he was real timid. Now he's not afraid of anything. He's calm and talks like any other person." From his cell, Pooler nodded assent.

Pooler's next cell neighbor, Leonard Arthur Pringle, 25, of Lancaster and Brooklyn, N.Y., has been reading the Bible to Pooler all week, and said a goodbye to him this morning.

Hears the Psalms

One of the last of the Scriptural passages that Pooler heard today was the 23rd Psalm, read by Chaplain Davis. Pooler said it comforted him.

The chaplain described Pooler as "A splendid fellow who made a mistake. I've never seen a man with so much faith."

The report also related that when guards came and took him to the execution chamber, that he twice shook his head in the negative when asked by Captain R. Fuller Goodman if he had anything to say.

Pooler was pronounced dead at 7:02 a.m., and he had died just two minutes and twenty-nine seconds after being strapped in the chair. The body was not claimed and within an hour he was taken to be buried at "Tickleberry." There the chaplains would pray and say a few meaningful words as the body of Willie Pooler was lowered into the ground.

Present with Chaplain Kelly that morning were the Reverend P. P. Belew, a Nazarene minister from Rochester New York who was a longtime friend and former district superintendent of the chaplain. Also present was the teen-aged Reverend William A. "Bill" Martin, a close friend and protégé of my father.

Martin went on to become Chaplain William A. Martin of the United States Army. And, when serving in Vietnam, he saw many examples of anguish and death while attending the needs of the wounded and dying. Nonetheless, in response to our request for him to share his impressions of the Pooler execution, Bill related that nothing had ever left him more troubled and profoundly overwhelmed than had that long ago electrocution of the youth from Darlington.

Chapter 28
Leonard Arthur Pringle and Ernest Willis

My father carried out his ministerial functions for killers Arthur Pringle and Ernest Willis as his last official death house duties on the morning of August 15, 1947. Governor Strom Thurmond had advised that his services were being terminated at the end of that month. And even though Dad felt it was his calling to tend the spiritual needs of those whose lives were to be taken, he was relieved that he would never again witness the mental torment of a fellow human being who was waiting for his life to be taken.

The two black men executed on that morning were each in their mid-twenties and the fathers of children. They were convicted of the robbery and murder of Willie Reid, a black taxi driver from the upstate city of Lancaster, on April 15 of that same year. The murder was brutal and both men had voluntarily confessed their guilt.

They were tried in July and on the tenth day of that month, they were found guilty and sentenced to death by Judge Arthur L. Gaston of Chester County. And it was only five weeks following sentencing when they took their last walks into the execution chamber to take their seats in the unforgiving chair.

The pair was from Brooklyn, New York, and they were in Lancaster visiting relatives when they decided to kill the driver who was lured into nearby Chester County and stabbed to death. After killing the hapless Reid, they took the one hundred and eighty dollars that was on him, stole the cab and buried his body.

Their escape attempt went awry and nothing worked as they had planned. Pringle was quoted by the *Columbia Record* as having said on the morning of the execution that, "Everything seemed to go wrong once we had killed the driver. Undoubtedly God meant for us to be caught."

Joy In the Death Cells

BOTH MEN EXPRESSED JOY and happiness before being put to death. And the chaplains stated that the pall of anxiety that often permeated the death house on execution Fridays was strangely missing.

The black chaplain, the Reverend E. A. Davis, is quoted as saying, "I never saw a happier pair of men in my life."

My father was also quoted as having said, "The two men were so happy that they wept tears of joy." Dad would also relate that the older member of the pair, Ernest Willis, had said, "I'll have breakfast in heaven."

My father returned from the death house that morning and called several of his clergy associates to tell them of the inspiring manifestations of faith he had witnessed before the two young men who were put to death an hour earlier. He related how they seemed to look forward to death and taking their spiritual journeys. My father's own belief was inspired by the Christian assurance that he had seen displayed in the death house that morning. He often referenced that execution in his sermons and when telling friends of his prison-related experiences.

Highly unusual on that morning was that the Reverend J. W. Shaw, a witness of the executions, was the uncle of Ernest Willis. Shaw told that Willis was born in Sumter County but that he had lived in New York from the time he was a small boy. He informed that the body would be claimed and that funeral rites would be held later that same day in Sumter.

Leonard Pringle's body was claimed by a local undertaker who prepared and returned it to his grieving family in New York for burial.

As a testament to their faith, the pair had been baptized on Thursday afternoon just hours before their executions.

The Final Moments

PRINGLE WENT FIRST AND had a prayer on his lips when the initial surge of the twenty-three hundred-volt current blasted into his body. He then received the follow up jolts that were routinely applied but sequentially reduced down to fourteen hundred- and six hundred-volt applications by executioner Sam Cannon.

Willis, upon taking his seat in the chair, asked Captain R. Fuller Goodman if he could have time to recite the 23rd Psalm. And his request was granted by the man who presided over all executions. In a voice that expressed an abiding faith and deeply felt emotions, the doomed man recited that comforting passage of Scripture. And he had a prayer on his lips when the current went racing into his strong body.

Willis did not die easily. Following the initial triad of high voltage electrical jolts, Dr. M. Whitfield Cheatham, prison physician, determined that Willis' heart continued to beat.

Executioner Sam Cannon then applied an additional series of jolts before he was declared dead. The elapsed time to snuff out the life of Willis had taken some five minutes and forty-seven seconds, the longest amount of time that Cheatham ever remembered for an electrocution. However, longtime executioner, Sam Cannon, stated that he could remember several executions that had required more than six minutes.

The slaying of Willie Reid was brutal and premeditated, according to the sheriff of Chester County. And the killers admitted that theirs was a crime that was planned and premeditated. As such, the murder aroused outrage among many of the cabbie's friends and relatives in Lancaster County. The newspaper also reported that, "A number of Negro men were in the audience today to observe the executions. One group of spectators watched Pringle die and was ushered out, and then a second group came in to see Willis die."

My Father's Departing Feelings

FROM THE EXECUTION OF Charlie Smith on November 29, 1946, through the executions of Ernest Willis and Leonard Pringle on that final morning of his death house chaplaincy, August 15, 1947, my father witnessed the deaths of fifteen flawed human beings, an unusually high number for a time span of just eight and a half months. His nerves jangled and he was exhausted. He recognized that he lacked the stamina to continue as chaplain, even before Governor Thurmond advised that he was being terminated. He understood that for his own well-being he would be unable to continue as chaplain and he was contemplating relinquishing that responsibility at the end of the year. Perhaps fortunately, Gov. Thurmond made that decision unnecessary.

My father and the Reverend E. A. "Lester" Davis, had done all they could to bring comfort and hope to murderers and rapists during their final hours. And even though Dad would cease witnessing Christ to condemned inmates, he felt relieved that he would never again experience the final moments of agony with doomed men and women as they awaited death.

In November of that same year, 1947, Dad was elected Church of the Nazarene district superintendent for the state of South Carolina, a church position that would have made it impossible for him to have continued to serve as chaplain at the penitentiary, even had Governor Thurmond chosen to keep him in that position.

The following chapter (Chapter 29) is the final chapter concerning the executions witnessed by my father. However,

Chapter 29 is not about death. It is about what my father described as a faith inspired 20th Century prayer miracle that spared the life of Joe Frank Logue, some seven hours before he was to be put to death on the morning of February 25, 1944. My father had only limited or no involvement in Chapters 30, 31, and 32. However, those chapters are significant to the history of crime in the state of South Carolina.

Chapter 29
The Miraculous Story of
Joe Frank Logue

Joe Frank Logue is mentioned frequently in chapters two and three and with good reason. As a highly regarded Spartanburg police officer and the indebted nephew of George and Sue Logue, the tall, athletic and personable Logue was pressured by his Aunt Sue and Uncle George to act as the bag man in their plot to hire a gunman who would kill store owner Davis Timmerman. Even though Timmerman was exonerated for the killing of Wallace Logue, who was the husband of Sue and the brother of George, the in-laws were determined that he must die to avenge the slaying.

Sue and George Logue and triggerman Clarence Bagwell had been sentenced to death in Lexington County due to their request for a change of venue. But, because of Joe Frank Logue's request to be tried in the county where Timmerman was slain, his trial was held in Edgefield County. Because of his being tried separately from the other three, he was not sentenced to die on the same date as his fellow defendants.

Even so, Logue was found guilty by a jury in Edgefield County, and he too received the death sentence. He would come within seven hours of taking his seat in the chair on the morning of

February 25, 1944, a date that fell some thirteen months following the electrocutions of his fellow conspirators, Clarence Bagwell and George and Sue Logue, who were all executed on January 15, 1943.

Fate, however, would save Logue from the chair in what my father called "A Twentieth Century Prayer Miracle." Dad would later write a small booklet, *If You Had Only 7 Hours to Live*. The booklet is an accounting of the prayer- and faith-inspired events that happened in the South Carolina death house at just minutes before midnight on February 24, 1944, and only seven hours before Logue was to have been executed at seven o'clock the following morning.

Five people had already succumbed to gunfire and three more had been executed because of the dispute between Wallace Logue and Davis Timmerman over three dollars, and Joe Frank Logue was to be the ninth and final victim of the mindless disagreement over the trivial sum.

The people of South Carolina had grown weary of the bold headlines and news coverage of the Logue case, and public opinion ran overwhelmingly against Logue. However, quite suddenly, public sentiment shifted, and all day Thursday the governor's office was inundated with pleas of mercy for Logue, who was to die the next morning.

From here, the events of that Thursday night in February of 1944 are quoted directly from my father's booklet. Dad would introduce the booklet to his audiences with the words that follow:

"It was for a long time that I had given this story not realizing that there was a text behind it. But one day while reading the Bible I ran across my text found in Psalms 102:19-20. 'For he hath looked down from the height of his sanctuary; from heaven did the Lord behold the earth; to hear the groaning of the prisoner; to loose those that are appointed to death.' So you see; this is a true scriptural message."

If You Had Only 7 Hours to Live
A Twentieth Century Prayer Miracle

By Rev. C. M. Kelly
Former Chaplain South Carolina Penitentiary

Governor's Visit

It was almost midnight Thursday when the governor and his staff drove up in front of the grey walls of the State Penitentiary to bring news to Joe Frank Logue of the commutation of his death sentence to life imprisonment. Joe was to have died on Friday morning so that is why I call this story seven hours to live, but let me give you a little insight to the story.

Eight People Die

Eight people are already dead because of an argument over a mule kicking a calf that belonged to Joe's uncle; the disagreement was to the amount of three dollars. Five people were shot down in cold blood murder and three others died in the electric chair. Being prison Chaplain at the time I spent the night with these three and witnessed their execution the following morning. But we wish to keep this story close by this man Joe as it is to be the faith inspiring message, we trust to the hearts of those who read.

Death Row

When Joe arrived at the prison and was put on Death Row, we had made up our minds not to become as seriously interested in him as we had the other three for our nerves were shattered in that terrible ordeal. But on our regular visit walking down the long corridor, a handsome man put his hand through the bars and said, "I'm Joe Logue. I guess you have heard of me," and I surely had for the three that died told me of how Joe had gotten them into this mess and then turned State's evidence, they said, "to save his own hide." I said, "Yes, and how are you?" He told me fine under the circumstance, and then gave me a most wonderful account of his conversion.

Converted In Cuba

It was in Cuba, a part of the prison where bad men are made to be good little boys on bread and water. He had been arrested for investigation and on his knees in Cuba promised God, "Live or die, I'll tell the whole truth," and then asked God to forgive him for not only that crime but for every sin in his life.

He then and there had a consciousness of sins forgiven, and took Christ as his Savior and Lord. At the trial he told the truth and was sentenced to die in the State electric chair February 2, 1943.

He also told me of a later Spiritual Crisis that came to him in the Edgefield jail, when some folk prayed for him and the Holy Ghost came in His fullness. He said, "He never doubted that the Holy Ghost abode in his heart." [sic] We talked a short while, and then made our way out of the prison until our next visiting day. On each of these visits we talked of the possibility of a life sentence for him, but I told him several times that public opinion was against him and that the Governor had said, "He would not interfere in the case." [sic] I talked to a member of the penal board and he said, "He's as good as dead. The public is tired of this feud. Eight people are dead and when they kill him they will end this whole bloody affair!" I never tried to build him up, for I knew he must make himself brave for this gruesome ordeal, but in spite of my pessimistic attitude he always said, "Well, I'm still trusting God." On one of my visits I saw tied to the back side of his cell, on what appeared to be the bottom of a cardboard box, heavily traced in pencil these words, "If ye abide in me, and my words abide in you, ye shall ask what ye will and it shall be done unto you." John 15:7. And I was told that this was the thing that he was depending on for his life.

I knew of course the Bible was true, but confess I was trying to figure some way of explaining this passage to his satisfaction, if he did go to the chair, so that he would not disbelieve the Bible. In other words I was trying to help God out of a tight place, but before this thing was over I learned that God could vindicate his truth without my assistance, and I needed to just preach the Bible, and God would take care of it being fulfilled.

A Distinguished Visitor

One day on my regular visit I saw the guard bringing two distinguished men into the hallway and I knew that they must be coming to visit Joe. I said, "I'll be back shortly," and went on down the way talking to several other prisoners, some that were also scheduled to die. I thought I recognized one of the men as being the governor's brother, and knew that he would probably have more influence with the Governor than any living person.

When they were gone, I went back to see Joe. I said, Joe did you ask the Governor's brother to help you?" He said, "I did not mention a word about him helping me. My faith is in God. I am depending on that verse John 15:7, if ye abide in me and my words abide in you, ye shall ask what ye will and it shall be done unto you."

On each visit I would tell him that from all I could see and hear he had better be prepared for the worst, as the public was strong against any kind of clemency. He would always say that God could overrule anything that anyone might do against him. If it came to the worst, he was ready to meet God, but if spared he would preach Christ to the prisoners.

Moved To Death House

Finally he was moved to the death house. He was the only occupant at that time so it was a lonely place, one man in a single cell, leaving five other cells empty. As I walked in the first day, Joe as all others who are sentenced to die seemed extremely nervous. I don't remember exactly how many days he had before his execution was scheduled, but it must have been about two weeks. This is about the usual time. There is a law that no man can stay in the death house less than three days or more than twenty-one. This law was made after Ed Bingham had spent more than forty months, being sentenced three times to die in the chair. At this writing he has been in the prison for over twenty-five years, still claiming his innocence. On one occasion he asked me, "Do you believe a man could murder his family, and keep the secret for over twenty-five years and still maintain his mental balance?" I will leave this question with the reader. His [Logue's] stay in the death house was just an ordinary occasion at the prison as someone is usually spending their last days there. I believe it was his last week when they had a hearing before the Supreme Court and at the end the case seemed to be just as it was at the beginning. One thing that impressed me was the terrible environment under which Joe had spent a great part of his life. During the whole time he said, "I'm guilty and according to justice I must die, but I am begging not for justice, but for mercy."

On one occasion a man was to be shot in Napoleon's army. His wife approached the Great General and asked for mercy. He said, "He deserves no mercy." She answered, "If he deserved it, it would not be mercy."

Two Days Left

Wednesday came and at ten o'clock P.M. the secretary of the State Pardoning Board went to the death house, took a seat and talked with Joe until midnight. They viewed the case from every angle and when he left, he later told me that he was convinced of Joe's guilt and said, "In my heart,

I said he must die." This was a dark hour in Joe's life, because without a recommendation from this board, a governor very seldom acts. He told Joe, "I won't give you any hope, as far as I know you will die Friday," so now only Thursday remained.

Twenty-One Hours of Prayer

When this dark hour came, it seemed that every avenue of escape was gone, except to look to God. I think to a certain extent he must have felt like Jesus in the Garden of Gethsemane when he said, "Could ye not watch with me for one hour," for at a time when he needed help as never before, all help seemed to fall away. It was then with a burdened heart and a desire for life he had laid his big Bible on the cement floor and placed his knees on it and began to pray. He said, "I had read the Bible on how God delivered Daniel out of the lion's den, and the three Hebrews out of the fiery furnace, without even the smell of fire upon them. I read of Paul and Silas being delivered out of the Philippian jail, and the Bible taught me that God was the same today as ever, Heb. 13:8. Jesus Christ the same yesterday, today, and forever. I prayed continually."

He said that he prayed uninterrupted for 21 hours, and probably most readers can't understand the deep feelings within a person who has one day to live. On Thursday there was a meeting of the pardoning board and the governor. I went to the governor's office but found so much excitement I decided it would do no good to stay for a visit, so I went home. Of course there was a dismal feeling within me because I had promised Joe that I would spend the last night with him should the worst come.

I can't recall all the events of that day but the things that happened on that night made a lasting impression on my mind. I left home about seven o'clock and told my wife that I would see her in the morning. We went to the prison and shortly were carried into the death house. When we stood in front of Joe's cell he stood near to the back wall, his Bible under his arm. He was extremely nervous and the suspense could be felt. He said, "I feel as good as could be expected, but it seems that man has turned me down, but even now God is able." We knew that a meeting had been held that day by the board but had not heard of the outcome. Joe was now pacing the short cell and groaning a prayer to God for help. I said to Rev. Roy Stewart who was with me, "Joe is so nervous he hardly knows we are here, so let's go back to the front office for a while." As we started out he called the guard who had been his keeper during his death house stay: "Tell me, have you heard anything?" The guard said, "Not a word, but when I hear I'll let you know." So we left him feeling something of the intense feeling of his pathetic heart.

Back in the front office we waited, with nothing to break the monotony except the old bell that would toll away another hour of a man's short life. At about ten o'clock we called the governor's office and the old janitor answered the phone. "Hello, is this the governor's office?" "Yas suh" was the reply, "but dey's no one heah but me, they left an hour ago." I said, "It's all over. He has turned Joe down or else he would come and break the news." I could only think of a lone man in a small cell, Bible under arm, waiting for news that from every earthly point of view would never come. Then at eleven o'clock the Associated Press phoned that the governor had commuted the sentence to life. I said in my heart "Glory to God." I wanted to run back to the death house and say, "Joe, your life has been spared."

But the governor's secretary said not to read the news until the governor comes, but it was the hardest secret to keep I have ever known. I wanted to go outside the wall and yell to the top of my voice, "Joe, your prayer has been heard," but all we could do was wait—but almost midnight the governor came, we went back to the death house and stood before Joe's cell.

The governor said, "Joe, do you have anything new to tell us?" Joe had been told that unless something new developed he must die.

Joe said, "Governor, if I have to tell something new, I will have to die. I have told the whole truth." The governor said, "I'll not keep you in suspense any longer, I've commuted your sentence." Joe looked dazed, stunned, baffled, then fell to the cement floor and said, "Jesus, Jesus, Jesus, Jesus, I thank you for saving my life!" Then he stood up and thanked the governor. There were tears in all eyes. I said, "It's time to pray," and as heads bowed, God came down into that old death house and it seemed that we were standing in the vestibule of heaven. When the prayers were over the governor said, "We must be going," I said, "Governor, I want to make one request: let's not leave him in here, let's take him out of the death house tonight." He said, "Sure." And the captain of the guard turned the lock. Joe picked up his Bible and as we walked to the door there came a big smile on Joe's face as he stepped into the yard. The very stars seemed to understand the great joy of one brought from death to life. Already passes had been given out for people to see the execution, but the old chair that had sent over 150 victims into that land from whence no traveler returns was robbed of its prey through the mighty weapon of prevailing prayer. So I believe He is still able to do exceedingly and abundantly more than we are able to ask or think. The extra paper with headlines reading "Logue's Sentence Commuted" was handed to Joe and he sat down to read. The governor said, "Preacher, you give the story to the papers. Tell them that some supernatural power entered this case." The secretary of the pardoning board said, "I left here Wednesday midnight determined that he must die. I went to bed but could not sleep." That was the same time that Joe was spending his twenty-one hours in prayer, and he added, "My mind was never changed, but my heart was changed."

The next morning at seven o'clock when he would have been making the last walk, Joe got down on his face and said, "Oh God, except for thy Grace I would now be taking my seat in the chair. Praise God for his wonderful Grace!"

Someone might say that Joe got "Penitentiary Religion," just something to save his life, but almost without exception the prisoners believe in Joe's religion. He always carries a big smile and a New Testament; teaches Sunday school and at every opportunity witnesses to the wonderful power of God.

Commutation Causes Controversy

THE COMMUTATION OF LOGUE'S death sentence created controversy and criticism of Governor Johnston. Elements of the press were vocal in their complaints, and one publication accused the governor of grandstanding for going personally to the death house to deliver the news that he had spared Logue from taking his seat in the chair. However, unknown to Johnston, it was his secretary who had given the word that Logue was not to be informed until the governor could come and tell the doomed Logue that his sentence had been commuted to a sentence of life.

Until his entourage arrived at the prison, the governor was under the impression that Logue had been given the news at around ten o'clock that evening when the press was advised that he had commuted the sentence. Then when he arrived at the prison at just before midnight, he was completely surprised to learn that Logue had not been informed and that they were waiting for the governor to personally convey the news to the man who was pacing the floor inside his cell in the death house.

My father felt the governor was treated unfairly by the press for the so-called grandstanding, and he contacted Johnston to ask permission to write a letter to inform the newspapers of the facts concerning the governor's visit to the death house. My father was told to use his own discretion as to the contents of the letter, and he wrote his communication in defense of the governor. The letter was published and the facts became known to the public.

Joe Frank Logue Becomes a Trustee

FOLLOWING SEVERAL YEARS OF incarceration at the main penitentiary, Logue then became a trustee at a prison facility just north of the city of Columbia. There he would use his boyhood skills of working with hunting dogs to train the state-owned bloodhounds. Logue trained the tracking dogs for a number of years as a trustee. However, once paroled, he was then employed by the state to continue his work of training and working the dogs.

My father would visit Logue during his years as a trustee, and he was often accompanied by his clergy associates and Nazarene Church officials who wanted to meet Joe Frank Logue, the man whose story so exemplified the power of prayer. Logue and other trustees would sometimes demonstrate the tracking abilities of the bloodhounds for the visitors by having the dogs locate one of Logue's fellow inmates. The trustee would walk into the nearby woods to walk in a flowing stream, climb a tree, or hide in some dense underbrush. Then, a half hour later, the dogs would be used to locate them. Everyone enjoyed hearing Logue's miraculous story and seeing the dogs at work. And the state benefitted from an unscheduled session of training for the sensitive-nosed bloodhounds.

The Reverend Hardy C. Powers, a general superintendent for the Church of the Nazarene, the denomination's highest office, would request to see Logue on his visits to South Carolina, where my father was, following his chaplaincy, district superintendent for the denomination in the Palmetto State. Powers received inspiration from Logue's story, and he always enjoyed his talks with Joe Frank Logue.

My Father Stays in Contact

MY FATHER AND LOGUE remained in friendly contact over the ensuing years until Dad's death in March of 1990. And even though they were almost the same age, Logue outlived my father by a number of years. Logue remained faithful to his conversion and never once did my father doubt his sincerity or his Christian commitment. Logue's wife, a devoted spouse and schoolteacher, remained loyal to him, and they enjoyed many years together after he was released from custody.

Chapter 30
The Captain Sanders Tragedy

The poignant saga of Captain J. Olin Sanders began on the Sunday morning of December 12, 1937. It was a routine Sabbath Day at the penitentiary, which meant that some of the prisoners would be receiving visitors while enjoying a day off from the usual work routine. And the staff of guards would have been reduced to the number of men needed to run the prison on such days of rest and relaxation. Captain Sanders was a highly regarded supervisor of the men who toiled as guards, and he was the man in charge at the prison on that cold Sunday morning in Depression era South Carolina.

The six convicts responsible for the murder of Captain Sanders had plotted their escape by taking the captain as their hostage, then demanding a car in which to flee while holding him captive until they had gotten well beyond the confines of the prison. Sanders was approachable, but he was not an easy foil for any inmate who was intent upon fooling either him or members of the guard staff. Unfortunately for the captain, he had the habit of leaving his office door unlocked when he was inside, a practice that would cost him his life.

From that ill-fated escape attempt that led to the murder of Sanders to the execution of the six conspirators some fifteen months later, the unusual and dramatic events involved in this case dominated the front page headlines in the Columbia newspapers. The infamous Sanders murder was state's most newsworthy crime of the 1930s, as had been the five Bigham family homicides during the 1920s and the Logue murders and executions in the 1940s. It seemed that, for three successive decades, once each decade, the small state of South Carolina was home to a crime of mind-boggling brutality. The added chapters provide a different human interest perspective to the narrative and are included for that reason.

The Attempted Escape

SEVERAL OF THE WOULD-BE escapees had plotted their actions for some three months prior to that ill-fated Sunday morning, the day picked for their escape. The six gathered in the mess hall where the inmates were having breakfast and from where they either singularly or in pairs crossed the prison yard to the captain's unsecured office. Their weapons were six homemade daggers and a realistic looking handgun that had been carved from wood.

Sanders was in his office when a member of the group attempted to engage him in conversation. The events that followed are not clear, but the escapees did somehow manage to seize the captain and take him hostage inside his office with its heavy doors and barred windows. There he was bound with rope and held captive for some three tension-filled hours as the prisoners made their demands and attempted to negotiate their release.

The superintendent of the prison, Colonel J. S. Wilson, went hurriedly to the prison where he immediately called the governor's mansion. Governor Olin D. Johnston was having breakfast at about eight o'clock on that Sunday morning, but when advised of the situation at the men's penitentiary, he rushed into action. He made an immediate call to his adjutant general and ordered him to bring out the militia. He then made his way to the prison, where he arrived just minutes after receiving the call from Colonel Wilson.

Upon Johnston's arrival at the prison, he learned that staff guards, Sergeant C. Wardlaw Moorman and Corporal Charlie Christmus, were already hunkered down and conducting negotiations from just outside the windows of the captain's office. The pair of guards had bravely volunteered their efforts to seek the release of Captain Sanders.

The governor took charge upon his arrival and within minutes he and the Reverend S. K. Phillips, then chaplain, walked across the wide drive to the besieged office and began negotiating with the would-be escapees. The courage shown by the governor and chaplain was reported widely in press reports and via the local radio stations as the negotiations were in progress.

The plotters were thought to be armed, and it was assumed that Johnston and Phillips were moving into harm's way, as had guards Moorman and Christmus, when they began negotiating the captain's release while standing outside the open office windows. The sextet of dangerous men stood firm in their mandate for a gas-filled car in which to escape, and it was reported they were requesting the captain's own personal automobile to make their get-away. They were adamant that the captain must accompany them but pledged that, if not followed, upon reaching a safe distance away from the prison, Sanders would be released unharmed.

For almost three hours the governor and the Reverend Phillips negotiated with the desperate convicts. And Adjutant General James C. Dozier arrived during the negotiations with a number of men belonging to the state militia. Johnston, bolstered by the presence of the men with Dozier, refused to yield to the demand for a car to be provided and neither side would budge from their positions.

The Governor Orders Tear Gas

JUST AFTER ELEVEN O'CLOCK, Johnston determined that negotiations were futile, and he ordered the use of both tear and nausea gas against the men who held the captain hostage. Dozier, a hero of World War I, and State Constable Frankie Meyer, a fearless law officer and former football star at the University of South Carolina, then took positions outside the open windows to stand and fire containers of the gases into the room.

State and prison officials later stated their belief that, prior to the use of the two gases, that Sanders had not been harmed. All six inmates would eventually confirm that the guard captain had indeed not been harmed until after the tear gas was used to rout them from the office. Several of the men stated that, even while sitting strapped in the chair, the guard officer had not been harmed, nor did they plan to harm him prior to their being assaulted with the gas canisters.

Once the convicts were routed from the office, the captain was found lying on the floor and bleeding profusely from five stab wounds. As the would-be escapees fled from the office, they were grabbed and beaten bloody by prison guards and national guardsmen. Following the beatings, they were stripped naked and stacked in a bizarre pile of living bodies for some minutes before prison trustees received the order to drag them to the infirmary to be treated for the effects of the gases that had forced their surrender.

A second group of guards and national guardsmen rushed to rescue the captain from where he had fallen on the floor and was at first thought to also suffer the effects of the tear gas. The guards hurriedly realized that he was mortally wounded, and they rushed to place him on a gurney and into a waiting ambulance. He was sped to the Columbia Hospital, but he died in the ambulance while en route to the emergency room.

The escape attempt was ill conceived and poorly executed. And none of the men had any plans beyond the immediate freedom they would achieve had their scheme been successful. Unfortunately, things turned deadly, and just two weeks following their escape attempt that had turned out a disaster, they were arraigned in the General Sessions Court in Richland County on January 10, 1938, on the capital offense of murder. Eight days later, on January 18, the trial began, and on January 22, less than a month following their crime, all were found guilty of murder.

Presiding Judge C. C. Featherstone imposed the death sentences on January 24 and set March 25 as the date on which they were to be electrocuted. Their court-appointed attorneys, however, began an all-out legal battle to save them from taking their walk into the execution chamber on the date specified by the judge. Due to the time consumed by the appeals, the original sentence had been delayed for almost a full year and the date of execution had been reset March 10, 1939. However, because of Governor Burnet R. Maybank's desire to study the case, the imposition of the death sentence was delayed for an additional two weeks and rescheduled for March 24, 1939, the day on which the six men were all put to death. Even though the wheels of justice were stalled for a year because of the appeal of the sentence, in that Great Depression era of the 1930s, when justice came swiftly, it had taken but fifteen months from the day of the murder to the date of execution.

The Cast of Characters

GEORGE WINGARD, A BAKER by profession, was the youngest and least hardened of the participants. Wingard, who was nineteen when executed, had already served three months of a year and a half sentence for housebreaking and larceny. With below normal intelligence, he had literally squandered his life to avoid serving the remaining fifteen months of his short sentence. He was from the Columbia area, and his supportive family lived nearby.

Herbert Moorman was the oldest of the group at forty-one and had been a plumber in Detroit, Michigan. He was serving a ten-year sentence for highway robbery and larceny in South Carolina. He was among several of the six with past records of fleeing custody. Moorman had previously escaped from prisons in Florida and his home state of Michigan. In Michigan, where he was a trustee, he had simply walked away from a prison while serving time for stealing chickens. Details of the chicken thefts are unknown, but many down and out individuals resorted to that practice during the Depression years of the 1930s.

It is interesting to note that the textile mills in South Carolina, a major source of employment in the state, were paying their workers an average wage of just thirty-two cents per hour during that era. For forty hours of hard labor in the mills, an employee could earn twelve dollars and eighty cents for his efforts. Many such people would plant gardens, own a cow, raise pigs, tend chickens, or shoot squirrels and rabbits to put milk, meat, eggs, and vegetables on their tables. And they canned or smoke cured much of what was produced to sustain them during the non-growing seasons. The act of stealing chickens was common, but it was not tolerated, as Moorman had learned while serving four to fifteen years in Michigan for breaking into a coop and stealing the hens that produced much of the protein in a working person's diet.

William B. Woods, alias William B. Gentry, was twenty-four and from Biloxi, Mississippi. Woods, a textile worker and one of the two who were married, was the most hardened member of the group and their self-acknowledged leader. Woods was serving a ten-year sentence on dual convictions for larceny and highway robbery, and he had already lost any and all time off for good behavior due to an escape attempt in January of 1937. However, his second attempt to escape that year came at the cost of his own and six other lives, including Sanders'.

J. V. Bair, also known as Jesse Williams, was twenty-seven, and his hometown was Sumter, South Carolina. Bair, a hardened criminal, was serving ten years for bank robbery and safe cracking in the city of Orangeburg. He was also serving a fifteen-year sentence for burglary and larceny in Florence County from where he had escaped. Following his capture in New Braunsfel, Texas, he was brought to the penitentiary on November 6, where he immediately joined the plot to escape.

Roy Suttles, a twenty-eight-year-old cotton mill worker from Simpsonville, South Carolina, was the second of the six who was married, and like his married counterpart, William B. Woods; he too was a hardened criminal. Suttles was serving a total of seventeen years for various infractions in the upstate city of Greenville. His convictions were for felony assault and battery with intent to kill, carrying concealed weapons, larceny, and highway robbery.

Clayton Crans, age twenty-nine, was a former bookkeeper from Rochester, New York. He suffered the crippling effects of childhood polio and was serving a two-year sentence for housebreaking in the Columbia area during September of 1937. In a similar situation to George Wingard, who would have completed his eighteen-month sentence only days before he was executed, Crans would have finished his sentence within a few brief months following his execution. Crans was recruited for the scheme just after he entered the penitentiary to begin serving his short sentence.

From the timelines, it appears that Woods, Suttles, and Moorman instigated the conspiracy and that Wingard, Crans, and Bair were persuaded to join them almost from the moment they entered the prison to begin their sentences. It is understandable that Bair, a hardened criminal, was a desirable addition to the plot. However, it defies understanding as to why Crans and Wingard, neither of them hardened felons, were sought out to join the plot or why they found the offer to join the real criminals desirable.

Drama Involving Governor Johnston

DURING THE NEGOTIATIONS FOR the release of Captain Sanders, it was observed that Governor Johnston had kept one hand in his overcoat pocket throughout the entire period of several hours. When asked why his hand had remained in his pocket, the governor responded that he was holding a pistol in that hand and that he would not have hesitated to use it, had it become necessary.

The would-be escapees were desperate and thought to be well armed, and it was assumed that all who were negotiating were risking their own lives and personal safety by volunteering to help free the captain. Even though it turned out that none of the inmates were in possession of firearms, the heroism attributed to Johnston and the brave rescue volunteers was never in question. All had acted with indisputable courage.

A Tribute to Captain Sanders

DURING THE 1930S AND '40s and perhaps today, there were inmates who were known as those who had been forgotten. They were inmates who were without friends or family and in whom society showed little interest. Johnston had a practice wherein he would solicit the input of prison officials, guard supervisors, and prison chaplains to identify the prisoners they thought to be rehabilitated and no longer posed a threat to society. For many such inmates, the governor, after a Pardons and Parole Board hearing, would grant paroles or early releases to those who were so identified as deserving. One such inmate identified by Sanders as among the deserving but forgotten was a Negro woman, Gertrude Stevens. Stevens had served twelve years of a life sentence following her conviction as an accessory to the murder of her husband. Sanders had designated Stevens as a well-behaved individual and had submitted her name to the governor with his recommendation for clemency. As a tribute to Sanders on the day of his funeral, which was attended by the governor and a multitude of state and prison officials, the governor paroled the forty-five-year-old Stevens, who already had a cook's job awaiting her on the outside, thanks to Sanders.

Drama and Unusual Happenings

WINGARD, CRANS, AND MOORMAN had been separated from the others and transferred to the Richland County jail to await the outcome of the appeal of their death sentence. While being held in that jail, the three somehow obtained a hacksaw blade with which they sawed through the cell bars during the wee hours of May 17, 1938. They managed to escape from the less secure facility and all fled into the early morning darkness.

An intensive manhunt was launched, and scores of police officers and civilian volunteers joined the search for the dangerous inmates. The search encompassed all of the city of Columbia as well as the swamps and wooded areas near the capital city. Late in the afternoon, Wingard and Moorman were spotted in the Crane Creek swamp that was just beyond the city's northern suburbs. They were apprehended immediately. However, the polio-crippled Crans did not limp from the woods until well after darkness had fallen. They were quickly transferred back to the solitary confinement area at the main prison to be confined in the dismal cells of Cuba.

The drama surrounding these three would remain a presence right up until they took their seats in the chair.

Execution Day Draws Near

JUST TWO DAYS BEFORE Wingard was executed, *The Columbia Record* ran an article that began with the sub headline, "Condemned Asks Right to Wed Girl." Wingard had fathered a child with his girlfriend, and the two of them desired to be married prior to his execution. The young woman visited her child's father in the death house just days before he was to be put to death, and even though Superintendent Wilson would have permitted them to marry, they decided against it, and she departed the prison as the unmarried mother of a soon-to-be fatherless child.

During the final week of life for Crans, Wilson told a man who sold supplies to the penitentiary of the soon-to-be executed inmate from Rochester, New York, also the vendor's hometown, whereupon the salesman asked to be taken to the death house and introduced to the doomed man. The visitor from Rochester did not know Crans, but he was familiar with the street and the area where Crans' mother continued to dwell. They talked for a while, and Crans was grateful for the time spent visiting with someone from his hometown. Both men seemed to enjoy their few minutes of conversation.

With the electric chair awaiting them on Friday, the polio-crippled Crans and fellow culprit, Moorman, the one-time chicken thief from Detroit, desired to make up for some of the pain that they had inflicted on their fellow humans. Both stated a desire for their bodies to be donated to any hospital that was interested and used for scientific study. Crans even offered to become a "living sacrifice" by donating his still-alive body to a scientific institution if it would be used to better understand his affliction of infantile paralysis. Their offers were rejected, but both Crans and Moorman continued to retain at least a small measure of conscience as the clock ticked away their final hours.

On January 19, 1939, some few weeks before William Woods was to be executed in March, *The Columbia Record* reported in a page one article that he had tried to kill himself. Woods, the acknowledged leader of the plot had somehow torn a piece of metal from his cot and had used it to slash both wrists in a desperate attempt to escape the chair. He was treated at the prison infirmary, kept overnight under heavy guard and returned to his cell the following day. There he was held under twenty-four hour surveillance until he was executed on March 24 of that year.

Ironically, it was a doomed fellow inmate who alerted the guards that Woods was attempting to commit suicide.

Drama continued to be a presence in this unusual case even as the doomed sextet was transferred from the solitary confines of Cuba to their cage-like cubicles in the death house. Such actions were a routine function at the prison, and such transfers were seldom reported by the press. However, due to the escape attempt that led to the murder of Captain Sanders, as well as the breakout from the Richland County jail by Wingard, Crans, and Moorman, in addition to Woods slashing his wrists, the authorities were taking no chances that something untoward might happen during the transfer of the six to the death house, and the press were invited to cover the move across the prison yard to the death house.

Both Columbia newspapers covered the transfer. *The State*, a morning daily, reported the inmates' move from Cuba to the death cells in its edition dated March 21, 1939, the day following the transfer of the doomed men. Following are excerpts from that report:

> The six doomed men in the Sanders slaying case took their last looks at the sun, the sky and the trees yesterday afternoon as they walked the 100 yard long pathway from their abodes of the last few months in "Cuba" to the death house at the state penitentiary.

> Only hours after Governor Burnet R. Maybank announced he would not intervene in the convicts' behalf, Prison Supt. James S. Wilson transferred the men to their death cells a few feet away from the electric chair in which they will die early Friday morning. The first electrocution is scheduled for 6:30 a.m.

After they had been transferred, Colonel Wilson read aloud to them Governor Maybank's decision on petitions of five of the doomed men for clemency. All except J. V. Bair heard it in silence. After the colonel had finished, the 29-year-old Sumter man laughed wryly and said, "Looks like that's that."

To Be Baptized

Some of the six men have expressed a desire to be baptized before they die. Colonel Wilson said this request would be allowed, but that the baptisms would take place inside the death house and not in the baptismal pool outside in the prison yard.

From "Cuba" To Death House

Five guards under Lieutenant Charlie Christmus surrounded each pair during the short walks. From watch-towers atop adjacent buildings other guards kept their rifles trained on the group. From a guard post just outside the interior prison yard fence, between which and the main cell block the silent group trudged, other blue coated members of the force remained on alert.

Bair, Wingard First

At 1:10 the first pair of convicts, Bair and Wingard, 20-year-old Columbian, handcuffed together, emerged from "Cuba," located at the rear end of the main hallway dividing the Richards building. They walked down the hallway, past the room in which Captain Sanders was stabbed. Then they stepped out of the hallway, through the same doorway through which they had staggered 15 months ago after they had been dislodged from Captain Sanders' office by a tear gas attack.

Guards halted the pair just outside the door, and they stood blinking in the sunlight, looking around curiously, with unfathomable grins on their faces. Then the entourage walked slowly across the prison yard in the sunshine, into the shadow of the small alley between the main cell block and the yard fence and down the short gravel walkway to the grim one story building that is the death house. A moment later, the death cell doors inside the structure had clanged shut behind them.

The guards returned for two more of the condemned men and at 1:15 emerged from Cuba with Roy Suttles, 29, of Simpsonville and William H. Gentry of Summerville, Ga., alias William B. Woods of Biloxi, Miss., confessed stabber of Captain Sanders and admitted ring leader of the plot.

Gentry Chews Match

Gentry nonchalantly chewed away on a match as the march across the prison yard started, his long lean jaw moving methodically. Expressionless, he surveyed a group of prison officials, newspaper men and civilians looking on. Suttles, grinning nervously, looked straight ahead.

Herbert Moorman, 42, of Detroit, Mich., and Clayton Crans, 29, of Rochester, N.Y., were the last of the six to be moved. Moorman's countenance was pale and drawn, Crans likewise as they trudged towards the death house. Moorman clutched a copy of the Bible.

After the six had been placed in their cells, Colonel Wilson went into the death house to read the governor's decision to them. As he entered the cell room and walked up the corridor on which the cells of Bair, Wingard and Crans faced, the thin tenor voice of Suttles from a cell on the other side of the room, slightly shaky, rose in the strains of the hymn, "Lead, Kindly Light."

Trio Expressionless

As Colonel Wilson started reading, Bair, Wingard, and Crans came to the front of their cells, leaning on the bars. Their expressions did not change and they did not move as Colonel Wilson went through the two page document.

When he concluded, Crans and Wingard remained stationary. Bair relaxed his intense grip on the cell bars, moved in a sudden nervous rush to one end of the cell, grinned in a wry manner and said, "Looks like that's that."

Suttles' singing had stopped a few seconds after the colonel started reading. When the prison head walked around to the other side (the cells are back to back, three facing east and three west) Gentry and Suttles said they had both heard all of it and there was no necessity of his reading the governor's decision again. "I missed the first part of it," Moorman said, his fingers clutching the front cell bars.

Gentry Lights Up

So as Gentry lay back on his bunk, silent and expressionless, and Suttles likewise, Colonel Wilson read the announcement once more for Moorman's benefit. Halfway through it, Gentry sat upon his bunk, pulled out a cigarette and loudly scratched a match on his shoe, the noise drilling through the silence that was broken only by Colonel Wilson's monotone. The convict lighted the cigarette, then lay back on the bunk again.

When the colonel finished, Bair asked to speak to a reporter.

"I just wanted to get the record straight," he said. "I've heard from two sources that the newspapers quoted me as saying, when the governor reprieved us the last time that I wished to God they would hurry up and get it over with. I didn't say that because that's against all Christian principles. Besides, I would never take the Lord's name in vain. My people might have read that and got the wrong impression."

Wingard had a piece of half inch ribbon tied around his head in the form of a wreath. His hair was neatly brushed and combed, and he said he kept the ribbon on to keep his hair in place.

Irony and Confusion

NEWS COVERAGE OF EVERYTHING involved in this case was extensive. However, at times, the reports were a bit confusing. The leader of the plot, William H. Woods, was also known as William B. Gentry. He was sometimes referred to as being from Biloxi, Mississippi, while in other news stories and references he was stated to be from Summerville, Georgia.

Ironically, George Wingard was more apprehensive about keeping the hair on his soon-to-be shaved head neat and orderly than he was with the more serious considerations facing him, even though he was only three days away from taking his seat in the chair.

Another bit of irony was that J. V. Bair, even though previously involved in felonies that ran the gamut from bank robbery to safe cracking and burglary, was more concerned about having his statements misquoted by the newspapers than he was over the crimes he had committed. He somehow reasoned that it was worse for his family to learn of his non-Christian utterances than what they already knew of his Christianity-defiant criminal actions. Whether his concern was for himself or was to lessen the worry for his family over his salvation, one can only speculate.

The Executions

THE MORNING OF MARCH 24, 1939, finally arrived and the sextet of prisoners were forced to pay with their lives for the murder of Captain Sanders. The executions went according to schedule, and news coverage was extensive. Pages of newsprint and photos were allocated to the story, and the following excerpts are from the afternoon edition of *The Columbia Record* following the executions that morning. Reporter Eddie Finlay wrote:

> Six men died calmly in the electric chair at the
> state penitentiary this morning—five of them firm

in their faith of salvation and the other without regrets.

The six and the order in which they died were George Wingard, 19, of Columbia and Batesburg; William B. Woods, alias William H. Gentry, 24, Biloxi, Miss.; Roy Suttles, 29, of Simpsonville; Herbert Moorman, 42, of Detroit, Mich.; Clayton Crans, 29, of Rochester, N.Y., and J.V. Bair, 28, of Sumter.

The crime for which they died was the slaying of Guard Captain J. Olin Sanders in an abortive prison break December 12, 1937, during which they held the captain captive in his office for several hours while demanding their freedom.

After all efforts to negotiate with the men had failed, tear and nausea gas was fired into the room and the men were routed out. Captain Sanders was brought out with five stab wounds in his body and died en route to the hospital.

When Sanders Stabbed

Every one of the six men declared this morning that Capt. Sanders had not been harmed until the gas was fired into the room.

The entire execution lasted only 48 minutes, Wingard being strapped into the chair at 6:30 and Bair being pronounced dead at 7:18.

All six were remarkably calm as they entered the death chamber through the little green door and walked over to the lonely chair in the center of the room—the same chair to which Capt. Sanders himself had led many doomed men.

Finlay then relates that even though hundreds of people had requested to witness the executions, Governor Maybank had ordered that only twelve individuals would be permitted to view the men as they were put to death. Included among the dozen official witnesses were two sons of Sanders, whom we will not name. Following are more excerpts from the news report:

> The witnesses were seated on a long bench, facing the chair while ministers and penitentiary officials were grouped to the right of the chamber.

> The condemned men could be heard singing as the witnesses approached the death house through the heavy morning fog. Guards had just finished their breakfast and impassive faced trustees watched the party as it filed through the yard from the main office. There was no sound from within any of the regular prison cells.

Call to Wingard

> As the chair was prepared for the first execution, the singing of the prisoners continued and as the officers left the death chamber for the first man—George Wingard—exclamations of "Goodbye, George—Atta boy, George," could be heard. Wingard entered the death chamber at 6:30, wearing a brown striped shirt open at the neck and grey trousers, split from the ankle to the knee on the right leg for the application of electrodes.

He was smoking but flipped the cigarette to the floor as he sat in the chair and the straps were adjusted by Capt. Claude A. Sullivan and other officials.

"Have you any statement to make, George Wingard?" Capt. Sullivan asked.

"Nothing except that the last statement I put out was true," the Lexington County boy replied. "My conscience is clear. I have made my peace with God and am ready to go."

Sticks to Statement

He was evidently referring to his statement of several weeks ago in which he retracted his trial testimony that Suttles had joined Woods in the stabbing of Sanders. At the time of his last statement, he said that his trial testimony had been based on the hope that he might receive a lighter sentence.

State Electrician, Sam Cannon, assisted by William H. Perry during the six executions, sent the first surge of 2,300 volts coursing through Wingard's body. As usual, the voltage was reduced for two additional applications, and Wingard was pronounced dead by Prison Physician I. H. Jennings in three minutes and twenty-two seconds. For this group of six executions, it was reported that Dr. Jennings had been assisted by Drs. O. L. Bruorton and W. S. Lynch.

Woods Grins at Death

The nonchalance that has marked his whole behavior since the morning that Capt. Sanders died remained with him to the end as he entered the room with a careless grin on his face.

He was chewing gum and smoking but spat out the gum as he sat in the chair.

As the straps were fastened he called out "so long" in a cheerful voice to a guard standing against the wall.

When asked by Capt. Sullivan if he had anything to say he replied, "Through perjured testimony five men have received injustice at the hands of the state of South Carolina.

"And you all know about this perjured testimony," he added looking towards Capt. Sullivan.

"Don't Choke Me"

After the mask had been placed over his face and as the cap was fastened over his head he remarked, "Don't choke me, boys."

He was pronounced dead in three minutes after the current was applied.

At the trial in January 1938, and at other times during the past year Woods sought to take the whole blame for Capt. Sanders' death.

Suttles was smiling as he entered the chamber and nodded to several of the spectators.

He made the longest statement of any of the six, saying like the others that Sanders had not been harmed previous to the firing of gas into the office.

Says Claims Innocence

"First, I want the people to know I have accepted Jesus as my savior," he said in a clear but slightly shaky voice. "I have made my peace and am ready to face God in the kingdom of Heaven where I know I am going.

"Second, I did not shoot Sherman Kelly in Greenville, the crime for which I was sent here." (Note: Suttles was sentenced for the wounding of Kelly, a Greenville policeman, in 1935.)

"Third, Capt. Sanders was not harmed before gas was fired into the room.

"Last, I ask Capt. Sanders' loved ones sitting over there to forgive me for trying to escape and so causing the death of their loved one."

He looked at Capt. Sanders' two sons as he said this.

"That's all. I am ready to go. God bless you all."

Three minutes and 59 seconds later he was pronounced dead.

Although all windows of the chamber were opened and a big fan was blowing through the room the acrid odor attendant on all executions had permeated the room. Most of the spectators were smoking and several had handkerchiefs held over the mouths.

Praise Prison Guard

"I have made my peace with God and I want to thank all officials, particularly Corporal T. B. Horton. The state is fortunate in having such a man down here," Moorman said as he sat in the chair.

The 42-year-old Detroit bookkeeper [sic] declared, like the others, that Capt. Sanders had not been harmed before the gas barrage and like the ones who had proceeded him showed no emotion. The executions were going off rapidly, four men having died by 6:58, only 28 minutes after Wingard entered.

(Author's note: The reporter was mistaken in calling Moorman a bookkeeper. Moorman was a plumber from Detroit, and Clayton Crans the bookkeeper from Rochester, New York.)

Clayton Crans, a slight, gaunt featured little man from Rochester, N.Y., was the fifth man to enter, limping on a leg withered by infantile paralysis.

"My only request is to shake the hand of Corporal Horton," he declared after he was seated in the chair.

Horton walked over and took his hand and the doomed man smiled up at him and, as the corporal stepped back, Crans said, "It was nice knowing you.

"I want to say crime does not pay," he said.

"Let all young men be warned by my example.

"I ask forgiveness of Capt. Sanders' family.

"I have accepted Jesus. May God forgive every one of you. May success and happiness be with every one of you."

Leg Hinders Electricity

As the cap was adjusted he began singing, "I'm Coming Home." The guards stepped back and he continued the hymn, "I'm Coming Home, Lord, and I'm Coming..."

His withered leg had made the application of the electrodes rather difficult and he was not pronounced dead until five minutes and six seconds after the current was turned on.

J. V. Bair of Sumter was the last to die. The other five had looked straight ahead but he glanced around the room as he sat in the chair.

"I feel terribly about Capt. Sanders' boys over there," he said in a low, clear voice.

"I have made my peace. I am ready to go.

"Tell all my loved ones, hello," he said as the mask was adjusted over his eyes.

"Do that, will you?" he added after the cap had been placed on his head and the guards stepped back.

Song Is Stopped

He began to sing "On Calvary's Cross" but was cut short before he had finished the first line. He was pronounced dead in three minutes, 34 seconds—only 48 minutes after Wingard had entered the chamber.

A heavy fog had risen from the bottom land around the penitentiary as the spectators left the death house and the sun shone like a golden ball through the haze. A knot of curious persons were peering through the bars of the main gate as the witnesses walked over to the main office to sign the death certificates.

The remarkable calm of five of the men was believed due to their having accepted religion during their long imprisonment but Woods' behavior was typical of his attitude ever since the trial.

Prison Chaplain S. K. Phillips and eight other ministers had spent the night with the doomed men after all but Woods had been baptized yesterday afternoon in the death house. Phillips revealed this morning that the other five had prayed long and earnestly for Woods to accept faith in God but he had refused.

The executions this morning constituted the largest mass electrocution for one crime in South Carolina penal history although six Negroes were electrocuted February 27, 1931—five of them for the same slaying. Before the electric chair was installed in 1912, more than six persons had been hanged for the same offense.

186 Die in Chair

The last man to die in the electric chair was George Gates, Darlington County Negro, who was executed December 9 for criminal assault upon a white waitress in the café in which he was employed.

Chapter 31
Ex-Soldier John K. Robinson and Zonnie Frazier

M y father was not officially serving as chaplain at the state penitentiary when Zonnie Frazier and John Robinson were executed on the morning of December 11, 1942, for unrelated murders. However, the Reverend W. M. Smith announced that he was tendering his resignation as chaplain and that his resignation would become effective on January 1, 1943. The date of Smith's departure was some weeks prior to when my father was to assume the chaplain's duties with the swearing in of Governor-elect Olin D. Johnston. The outgoing governor, R. M. Jefferies, asked Dad to assume the role a bit early, and he then became indirectly involved with the executions of Robinson and Frazier before his duties would become official.

My father did not witness those two executions, but at the invitation of Chaplain Smith, he accompanied the outgoing minister on several visits with the doomed pair in the death house. The personality contrasts between the inmates are revealing and are worthy of narrating as a part of Dad's prison experience, even though he was not officially involved.

The following accounts of the executions of John Robinson and Zonnie Frazier are reconstructed from the archives of *The Spartanburg Herald* and *The Columbia Record*.

Crime Committed by Robinson

JOHN K. ROBINSON, TWENTY, from Ottawa, Illinois, was serving as an army corporal at Camp Croft in Spartanburg when he committed the brutal murder of middle-aged taxi driver, Kenneth J Wofford, also of Spartanburg. Wofford was shot to death on January 4, 1942, out on a country road near Pacolet Mills with robbery as the motive. Both Robinson and his wife, a young Spartanburg woman he met while stationed at Camp Croft, were present at the shooting.

The case was complicated, but Robinson's testimony and a lack of evidence that his wife was involved prevented her from being charged, and she would go on to deliver a stillborn baby in October. Obviously, she became pregnant at about the time of the robbery and murder of cabdriver, Kenneth Wofford, and her days of nerve wracking trauma were believed to have contributed to the death of her baby.

Robinson was twice tried for the murder, and the first trial was held in January of 1942, the month in which the crime was committed. After twenty hours of deliberations minus a verdict, a mistrial was declared. Robinson was tried a second time in April, and after only fifty-five minutes of jury deliberations, he stood convicted of murder with no recommendation for mercy.

The verdict was challenged and the appeals process delayed the execution until December. Nonetheless, during that era when justice came swiftly, John Robinson murdered a man in January and was executed eleven months later in December, even after he was provided with two separate trials and the sentence delayed by his appeal.

Robinson's Personal Plea

WITH HIS EXECUTION LESS than two weeks away, Robinson appealed directly to Governor Jefferies to spare his life. Following are excerpts from *The Spartanburg Herald* edition of December 5, 1942, in which Robinson is quoted directly:

> "I have a fierce pride but I'm putting it aside now to beg you for mercy and a chance to live and love and do all of the things that come with life.
>
> "I'm not as hard and cruel as some people make me appear. They know that I'm human and not a vicious, blood-thirsty animal as the solicitor put it somewhat strongly in his summary before the jury.
>
> "If you would give me a chance to live, perhaps sometime the authorities may see fit to release me, allowing me to go free, free to repay my wife for the love and loyalty she has shown; free to make up for the dishonor I have brought my people's good name."

From *The Spartanburg Herald*

> In reviewing the events leading up to Wofford's death by the side of a highway near Pacolet, Robinson said his nerves were on edge and that he was "taut" because of his unsuccessful efforts to be transferred from Camp Croft, where he was training troops, to a combat zone. He said he had planned to leave the state in Wofford's taxicab, which he intended to commandeer.
>
> "He (Wofford) was walking off at last, after at least three minutes of discussion that took place

beside the parked taxicab," Robinson told the governor. "My wife sat on the back seat, quiet and astonished at my actions. I lowered the gun as I started to turn to get in the car. As I turned, he cried out and started to run. He startled me so bad that I jerked all over and the gun went off. How I hit him at all from the position of the gun is something I don't know."

Second Shot Mercy

"The only reason I can give for shooting him a second time is 'complete frustration' and an act of mercy. He was groaning horrible as I ran to him to raise his shoulder. I could see the blood on his chest in the side beam of the car's headlights before he squirmed out of my grasp. It sickened me awfully and I clamped my jaw hard and fired again."

Robinson's Appeal

In the Robinson case, Governor Jefferies released for the first time several portions of the ex-army corporal's appeal of a week ago, in which he gave for the first time his version of the shooting of Wofford.

The governor said, however, that he had read the court and other records, had heard the personal appeal of Robinson's wife, a request for clemency from a chaplain at Camp Croft, and "particularly, the very pitiful appeal made by your (Robinson's) foster parents"; and still was unable to extend clemency.

"From your own statement, the crime you committed was a horrible one," Governor Jefferies said in his reply to Robinson's appeal.

"I can find no extenuating circumstances that would warrant a reduction of the sentence of the court. As a result of your action, a good man's life has been taken and his family left in sorrow. Society has been injured.

"The Law is definite."

Zonnie Frazier

ZONNIE FRAZIER, NINETEEN, WAS convicted and sentenced to death for the murder of Charles Dubose, a Lamar police officer who attempted to place him under arrest in a "Negro establishment" in July. The case received little publicity, and not much information on Frazier was uncovered during our search of the records concerning his crime and execution. However, due to my father's minimal involvement with Frazier, this narrative is confined to the human interest aspects of his execution, which are most interesting.

Ironically, in addition to sixty-six-year-old Charles Smith in chapter fifteen and twenty-eight-year-old Lewis Scott in chapter seventeen, Frazier was the first of the three black men with whom my father was somehow involved to be executed for killing a law enforcement officer who was attempting to place them under arrest. In each of the three slayings, alcohol was a factor and none of the murders was premeditated; all were spontaneous. Drunkenness was directly responsible for three senseless murders and three subsequent executions.

Reported by The Columbia Record

THE COLUMBIA RECORD REPORTED the executions in its afternoon edition dated December 11, 1942. Frazier and Robinson had died in the chair that morning, and excerpts of the article by Eddie Finlay are descriptive. Excerpts from the report are as follows:

> A defiant former soldier with "nothing to say," and a quiet little Negro whose "soul was saved" died calmly in the electric chair at the state penitentiary this morning.

> The ex-soldier was John K. Robinson, 19, former corporal at Camp Croft, and the Negro was Zonnie Frazier, 19-year-old Darlington County farm worker.

> Frazier died first, entering the death chamber quietly and stepping calmly into the slightly raised chair. He watched the guards curiously while the straps were adjusted and when asked by Guard Captain Claude A. Sullivan whether he had anything to say, smiled and answered, "I feel good, feel good. My soul is saved."

> Captain Sullivan then asked him what he had done with the gun used in killing the officer and he said that he had given it to his uncle.

> He was pronounced dead four minutes and thirty-seven seconds after state electrician Sam Cannon had turned on the current. A second shock was necessary after examination showed that his heart had not stopped beating. Cannon said this was an unusual thing and only the second time he had seen such an occurrence.

Zonnie Frazier died expressing that his soul was saved. Robinson, though, was an atheist and firm in his belief that God did not exist. Frazier felt he would be in heaven from the very instant of his death. In sharp contrast, John Robinson believed he would spend eternity decomposing in his grave.

Robinson Executed

Robinson, a professed atheist who had turned down all religious solace offered him, showed little emotion and declined making any last statement, telling Captain Sullivan, "I have nothing to say."

He was pronounced dead three minutes and 47 seconds later.

Many See Electrocution

The little death chamber was almost filled with witnesses, including several soldiers from Camp Croft and two women, who came in after Frazier had been electrocuted.

Guards and ministers who had talked with the two condemned men in the death house said that Frazier, who was baptized several days ago, had endeavored to convert Robinson but had failed. The two had shared their cigarettes and frequently sang together, staying up most of one night singing "The Darktown Strutters' Ball."

Robinson had kept his belief to the last, refusing to talk with ministers and even asking guards to keep them away from his cell.

The Rev. W. M. Smith, prison chaplain, said that Robinson was sleeping soundly when several ministers came to his cell around 6:30 this morning and turned down an offer of baptism because, "the water's too cold."

The Spartanburg Herald Coverage of Robinson's Execution

THE UPSTATE NEWSPAPER DID an excellent job of covering the execution of John Robinson with two separate accounts of the electrocution on Friday, December 11, 1942. The *Herald* edition that hit the streets on Saturday morning featured reports by *Herald* Staff Correspondent Glen W. Naves and City Editor Vernon Foster. Naves wrote:

With a grim smile and two low but firmly uttered "Okays," young John Robinson embraced the death angel in the South Carolina state prison at 7:45 o'clock this morning.

Robinson, former army corporal at Camp Croft, walked to the electric chair unassisted. He seated himself in the structure of wood and steel. The straps and mask were adjusted and the current turned on.

In two minutes and 47 seconds he had paid with his life for the gunshot slaying of Kenneth J. Wofford, elderly Spartanburg taxicab driver, on a lonely Pacolet community highway Sunday night, January 4, 1942.

Prison Chaplain W. Monroe Smith walked with Robinson from his cell to the chair. There he asked the condemned man, "John Robinson, do you have anything to say?"

No Statement

Seated, Robinson looked to the right, glancing slowly about a section of the crowded room. He smiled and replied: "I've got nothing to say!"

Robinson hesitated briefly before speaking. He did not speak again.

Two or three seconds before he smiled as the straps were adjusted about his chest and arms, he uttered two "Okays"—split seconds apart in a low voice as the straps were adjusted.

Stoic to End

The stoicism which surrounded his slender body like armor plate and steeled his spirit from the time of his arrest until his soul was shocked into eternity did not desert him for a moment. Unemotional, uncomplaining and impassive he sat in the chair with his hair clipped and his head shaved—but unshorn of courage.

Funeral Held Here

With only a small company of relatives and friends attending, funeral services were held at the graveside in Carlisle Church cemetery in Spartanburg County this afternoon at 3 o'clock.

(AUTHOR'S NOTE, THE FUNERAL was held on December 11. Ironically, the atheist's remains would be buried in a church cemetery, an institution he so disdained while he lived.)

The body was brought to Spartanburg in a J. F. Floyd mortuary ambulance. Attaches of the funeral home arrived at the prison before dawn, waited until the execution was ended and then received the body.

The death chamber was quiet as a tomb as Robinson walked in and took his seat in the chair. Disregarding the opportunity to make a statement, he signified that he was ready to die. His chest and arms were strapped in to the chair. The death mask was placed over his eyes. Stepping to the huge switchboard behind the chair, Sam Cannon, veteran electrician at the penitentiary who has officiated at dozens of electrocutions, threw a switch.

Robinson stiffened as the heavy voltage tore through his limbs and torso. His body was raised about three inches out of the chair. Lights on the switchboard panel flickered and the youth sank back into the chair. The switch was thrown a second time and again the shock raised him up from the wooden seat.

Asked no Quarter

Stepping to Robinson's side, Mr. Cannon pulled out a watch. Dr. M. Whitfield Cheatham [sic], prison physician, unbuttoned Robinson's shirt. He applied a stethoscope to the chest area over the heart. There was a pause of several minutes. Somewhere in the group of spectators two men began talking. Someone laughed. A guard rapped sharply on the floor. "Quiet, please." Dr. Cheatham [sic] stepped back. "All right," he said.

Robinson's body was unstrapped from the chair as the 40 odd spectators, including several soldiers and two Columbia Hospital nurses filed out.

Rigid and still in the sitting position, Robinson's body was carried out by two Negro men. His eyes were closed. His head was slumped to the side. Immobile as was his body after the current shot through it was Robinson's fortitude as he came to the end of life in his 20th year; he asked no quarter with death and he gave none. Neither did he express any regret over the crime for which he died. Steadfastly he refused all offers of spiritual counsel and guidance.

Visited by Minister

Early this morning the Rev. J. B. Stepp, pastor of Selma Baptist Church in the Woodruff section, accompanied by Chaplain Smith, visited Robinson in his cell. Discussing his experience with the prisoner, the kindly bespectacled minister said, "Robinson was asleep when I entered his cell at about 6:30 o'clock. He had his head covered up. We had to awaken him. He was wearing pants and a shirt. He got up and put his shoes on."

"I talked with him. I begged him to accept Christ as his personal Saviour. He refused."

"He said, 'If you have got to sing, go ahead. I've got to wash my face.' Then he turned his back to us. I have talked to hundreds of men about their spiritual welfare as a minister. He was the coldest man I have ever talked with. He could not be reached. Finally, he told me, 'I am an atheist.' I read to him portions of two chapters in the Bible from St. John and Ephesians. He said, 'I don't believe that stuff.' I remained and saw him die. There was no way to reach him."

Vernon Foster Report in The Spartanburg Herald

VERNON FOSTER DID NOT write as extensively of the Robinson electrocution as did Glen Naves, whom he accompanied to do their dual coverage for the newspaper. However, even though both reported what they saw that morning, there are informative and human interest differences in how they viewed and reported the execution. Foster wrote:

Death in any form is not a pleasant thing to see but after witnessing my first execution this morning, I am convinced that as long as the law demands a life for a life the electric chair is the most humane instrument of justice.

Together with about three dozen other official witnesses, I watched John K. Robinson, a 20-year-old convicted murderer from Spartanburg County, pay the supreme penalty today for the slaying of Kenneth J. Wofford, elderly Spartanburg taxicab driver.

First Experience

It was my first opportunity to view an execution and it has been suggested that my reactions and feelings might be of some interest to the public.

Our party arrived outside the high, iron barred gate of the South Carolina penitentiary this morning shortly after 6 o'clock. It was still dark, but inside the gates a small group of men in civilian garb were gathered in a knot under glaring floodlights.

Identification was quickly established at the gate and we moved inside for a brief talk with G. R. Richardson, superintendent of the penitentiary. Three members of our party of newspapermen and soldiers already had official passes for the electrocution of Robinson but Mr. Richardson expressed some doubt that room could be found in the narrow death chamber for others in the group.

"Go inside and have some breakfast," he advised, "and we'll see what we can do."

In the guards dining hall, two great platters of piping hot biscuits; a large cake of butter; a deep bowl of steaming grits and plates of sausage—made at the state prison farm—waited for any and all visitors. Trustees quickly brought mugs of hot coffee for the entire group as we entered the room.

Others Are Guests

Already seated at the table were two prison guards and two other men from Spartanburg (names omitted by author), both of the J. F. Floyd mortuary.

Between buttered biscuits, table talk naturally swerved to the approaching execution of Robinson.

"What's he having for breakfast?" a newsman inquired. "He's not asked for anything for breakfast," was the reply of one of the trustees. "But he ate a whale of a supper last night: T-bone steak, French fries, and two hunks of apple pie and chocolate ice cream." "How's he seem to be taking it?" One of the guards replied, "Oh, easy enough. He doesn't seem to be worried." The other guard, a quiet middle-aged man with captain's insignia on his shoulders, looked up and smiled.

"A Tough One"

"He's a tough one all right." I learned later that he was Captain C. A. Sullivan, the officiating officer at all executions.

A trustee popped his head inside the door. "All you newspaper guys are wanted outside!" he called.

Outside it was still dark. We grouped around a guard sergeant near a gate to the inner wall.

"You fellows who are going in to see the Negro line up over here," he ordered. In the line that quickly formed were about 25 men, including several law enforcement officers and four army officers—one a colonel.

Quickly, the line of men was marched inside and the gate banged shut. The witnesses disappeared from sight around a corner, and the rest of us lounged against a fence and tried to keep warm. Superintendent Richardson happened along, stopped for another chat and volunteered the information that it was all right for our entire party to go inside the death house for the next execution.

Leaves Hurriedly

"One side there!" someone called and we looked up to see the gate opening for the army colonel. His face was a sickly grey in color, and he walked hurriedly towards the prison offices.

"The Negro's already knocked off, I imagine," observed one veteran newspaper man.

Sure enough, at that moment, the witnesses for the execution reappeared. They had been gone only about five minutes.

"Sergeant, here are two ladies who will witness the next one," called a clerk from the office porch. Men in the line looked quickly around on the chance that the two women might be related to Robinson. But Superintendent Richardson passed the word along that both were nurses at the Columbia hospital.

A moment later, we were being marched towards the low-ceilinged brick building inside the inner fence that houses the chair of death. Hardly had we passed inside until the door closed behind us, and four guards walked through an inner door, the condemned man in the center of the group.

He didn't even look at the crowd, just gazed curiously at the chair in the center of the room. He grinned faintly.

Spurning assistance, he seated himself in the chair and then looked around the room. Matches flared as cigarettes were lighted by about half the men in the room.

At that moment, Robinson appeared as calm as any man in the room.

Foster then goes on to describe the execution in much the same manner as had his associate reporter, Glen Naves. However, the final paragraphs in Foster's narrative are worth sharing. Foster continued:

The entire execution had consumed barely five minutes. At the door I looked back. The mask had been removed from Robinson's face. The mouth had been pulled wide apart; the eyes bulged. It was not a pretty sight. But, as I left the death house, instinctively, my memory carried me back to the night of last January 4, when I accompanied the sheriff's officers to the lonely country roadside where the pitifully sprawled body of a harmless old taxi driver had been found in a ditch. His face was buried in a mass of bloody mud; a gaping wound had been inflicted in the back of his head; and a jagged blood-encrusted hole was found in his chest. Beneath his outstretched hand, a few miserable pennies, nickels and dimes were scattered. That wasn't a pretty sight either.

AUTHOR'S CONCLUSION: THE ARTICLES in *The Spartanburg Herald* by Glen Naves and Vernon Foster provided unique and thorough accounts of the execution of John Robinson. Via their superb skills as newsmen, they captured the horror of the crime and the emotions that are present when the life of a badly flawed human is taken by the brutal chair. By using excerpts from theirs and the Eddie Finlay article in *The Columbia Record*, we have attempted to take the reader inside the minds of both those being executed as well as those who witness the taking of a human life.

Chapter 32
The Bigham Family Tragedy

One of the more infamous cases in the criminal history of South Carolina involved the Bigham family murders. Ed Bigham was the son, sibling, and uncle of the murdered quintet of Bigham family members and he was charged with the slayings. He was tried and sentenced to death by electrocution at three separate trials during the 1920s.

At his fourth trial in 1927, Ed accepted a life sentence in exchange for a plea bargain. As a result, he would escape sitting in the chair that was in the room adjacent to the death house cells where he spent so many months awaiting his own execution. During his prolonged confinement in one of the six tiny cells, it is said that Ed Bigham bade farewell and watched as some thirty-three men took their final walk into the bleak chamber, where the electric chair was used to take their lives.

Once his plea bargain was accepted and he no longer felt at risk of being executed, Bigham would immediately and steadfastly deny the five family murders, a position from which he never vacillated right up until the moment of his death from natural causes some decades later. He died a free man some few years following his parole in 1961.

The Bighams were a prominent family in Florence County, and Ed Bigham's father had once been a formidable South Carolina state senator. In much the same manner as the Logues in chapter two, the Bighams were large property owners who were involved in the business of harvesting timber and milling it into lumber.

The slayings were thought to have occurred between two and three o'clock on the afternoon of January 15, 1921. Ed's mother, sister, his brother, and his sister's pair of adopted sons had all succumbed to gunfire on that date, except that one of the young boys clung to his life at a hospital until around five o'clock the following morning.

Bigham and Logue Crimes Comparable

THE HOMICIDES WERE THOUGHT to have erupted during or over a family dispute involving seventy-five thousand dollars, a substantial sum of money during the 1920s. However, the insane Logue-Timmerman conflict over a paltry three dollars, some two decades later, during the early 1940s, would prove to be even more deadly than was the quintet of Bigham family murders.

Five people were gunned down in each of the infamous quarrels but for different reasons and enormously diverse sums of money. In both cases, an additional person was sentenced to die but escaped execution to begin serving a life sentence, a penalty from which they would ultimately be paroled. The Logue case, in addition to five individuals being murdered, also resulted in three executions, including Sue Logue who was the first woman ever electrocuted by the state of South Carolina. The similarities in these cases are striking, and it is ironic that my father was involved in both history-making settings, separated by some two decades.

My Father Becomes Involved

THE AUTHOR MANAGED THE F. W. Woolworth Company store in the city of Florence during the 1959-60 time period when South Carolina State Senator Ralph Gasque secured a hearing before a judge in Florence County in the senator's attempt to free Ed Bigham. I attended the first hearing, which did not go well, and the prosecutor was adamant that he would resist any attempt to retry or release Ed Bigham under any condition.

I had personally met Bigham during visits to the prison with my chaplain father some fifteen or more years prior, and I remember that my father would stop for a few minutes of pleasant conversation with the courteous old inmate whose work assignment was to feed and care for a couple of pet deer that were kept in an enclosure inside the prison yard. In consideration of his age and the fact that he had lost part of an arm in a railroad accident before becoming an inmate, Ed Bigham was given the light duties of caring for the rescued animals, a chore he seemed to enjoy.

During a break in the court proceedings, I informed Senator Gasque of my father's involvement with Bigham at the prison, and I shared that my father, who was then pastor of the First Church of the Nazarene in Raleigh, North Carolina, would be pleased to come and render whatever assistance he could as a character witness for Ed Bigham. The senator was pleased with the information, and he soon contacted the former chaplain to come and testify at a parole board hearing scheduled for a later date.

My Father's Testimony

FOLLOWING THE PAROLE BOARD hearing, during which Ed Bigham gained his freedom after some thirty-nine years as an inmate, reporter Eugene Fallon, who himself testified in Bigham's behalf, wrote a column on Bigham's release for the Florence *Morning News*. Following are excerpts from the Fallon Column:

> A six man parole board, after hearing pleas of
> State Sen. Ralph A. Gasque and his law partner
> William H. Scales, Marion attorneys, and two

character witnesses, by a vote of four-to-two flung open the door of liberty for convict Edmund D. Bigham yesterday morning.

Bigham, accused of wiping out his family in a blood-bath at the family homestead in lower Florence County in 1921, thus won liberty after more than 39 years spent behind bars and following several close brushes with death by electrocution. The board deliberated only briefly after the hearing before handing the aged convict his passport into a world that has all but forgotten his existence. Notified of the decision, Bigham bowed his head and his lips moved as if in prayer. He had to be assisted from the building. Outside in the glare of midday, Bigham trembled visibly.

One of the character witnesses heard by the board was [the] Rev. Charles M. Kelly, Nazarene minister from Raleigh, N.C. Mr. Kelly who had come to South Carolina at his own expense, served as prison chaplain at Columbia some years ago and had often talked to Bigham. The minister reiterated his belief that Bigham "harbored no resentment against anybody" and was, in effect, an "excellent parole risk."

The writer also spoke in the longtime convict's behalf, pointing out that Bigham, regardless of his guilt or innocence of the crimes with which he had been charged, "had spent more time behind bars than any man in the history of the state" and that it was his conviction that the majority of the people in Bigham's home county (Florence) felt that the aging convict had paid his debt to society and was entitled to die away from prison bars.

Later, after he had had time to recover his composure and when he was surrounded by a battery of newsmen, Bigham drew strength from joy. Tilting his cane once or twice in a manner almost debonair, the liberated lifer answered every question posed with a cleverness that belied his age and the gray weight of two-score years behind prison walls.

The following excerpts are from a page one news report in the same issue of the Florence *Morning News*:

Five men tramped down the corridors of the South Carolina State Penitentiary, two lawyers, a newsman, a prison official and the most notorious convict in the Big House.

Edmund Bigham, convicted murderer from Florence County, needed no guide. The dreary corridors have known his despairing footsteps for 40 years!

Bigham needed no guard either. He has just won parole. The old man spoke: "Senator Gasque," he said suddenly. "I never gave much thought before to Abe Lincoln's Emancipation Proclamation... But now I know how those poor souls must have felt. I am free! Free as a bird!"

Through that mysterious form of communication peculiar to prisons and known as the "grapevine," all the convicts knew Ed Bigham would be leaving in a matter of hours. All looked at him; from their cells they peered and in the walkways they turned and craned their necks. Strangely enough, there seemed to be no envy in the glances. Old Mr. Bigham, they knew, had served out his time.

On the Third Tier the party halted. With almost a flourish, Bigham waved us into his cell, a tiny cubicle, seven by nine feet. A great old fashioned radio was there. Edmund said proudly that it held sixteen tubes. It was his own. Other than some pitiful cardboard boxes neatly stacked against a wall, the rest of it belonged to the state of South Carolina, the cot with its thin mattress, the lone window, and the bars which cut off the world. There was a cheap metal trunk. It was carefully packed, bare as the cupboard of Mother Hubbard. Bill Scales, Marion attorney, bent over and inspected the cardboard boxes. They were all carefully addressed: "To E.D. Bigham, Marion, S.C."

"You must have had faith in being released by the parole board," Scales told Bigham.

"I knew the Lord realized that I had been tormented enough," came the reply. "He also knew I was weary of waiting, waiting, waiting."

The various articles went on to explain that Senator Gasque and his law partner, attorney Bill Scales, had worked without charge in behalf of Bigham and that Gasque had a light duty caretaker's job and a small apartment across the hall from their law offices lined up for the old man who had spent so much of his life as a prisoner.

During our research it was learned that there were no witnesses opposed to Ed Bigham being paroled. During my father's testimony he told that, "Bigham asked me once if a man could kill his brother and his sister and stay in prison for 25 years and retain his mental balance. I told him that would be hard to do." My dad related that, "Bigham was a nice fellow and I always liked and respected him."

Authors Note: At least one book has been written on the Logue-Timmerman feud and the Bigham murders. The Bigham family tragedy is narrated in *A Piece of the Fox's Hide* by Katherine Boling, Sandlapper Publishing Inc. The Logue story is told in *The Guns of Meeting Street* by T. Felder Dorn, University of South Carolina Press.

About the Author

Charles Wesley Kelly was born in August 1931 and graduated from Olympia High School in Columbia, South Carolina, with the class of 1950. Following several semesters at the University of South Carolina, he was called to active duty with the Navy and assigned to the *USS Cowell*. The ship (DD 547) was a re-commissioned World War II destroyer that had earned eleven battle stars in the Pacific Theater of operations and a Presidential Unit Citation at the battle of Okinawa.

The ship then received an additional two battle stars for action during the conflict in Korea and was running carrier escort duties when the ceasefire agreement was reached in June of 1953. The author was discharged in September following the long voyage home during which the ship was dispatched to show the flag in numerous ports, all the way from Japan up through the Suez Canal and on both sides of the Mediterranean, before arriving at its home port in Norfolk, Virginia.

He then went to work for the F. W. Woolworth Company in anticipation of returning to school the next semester. However, he was persuaded to become a management trainee for the iconic five and ten cents retailer and never returned to the university to complete his studies to become an attorney. Progressing through the store management and executive ranks of the corporation in assignments that took him to live in six different states and thirteen cities, he ultimately became vice president for the Foodservices Division of Woolworth USA at the corporate headquarters in New York City. While filling the assignments at the corporate headquarters, he was instrumental in converting twenty-two Woolworth lunch counters and coffee shops into highly successful Burger King franchised operations.

He transferred back to the Woolworth Southeastern Regional Office in Atlanta in 1987, and he continues to live with his wife, Kathy, in the suburban Atlanta community of Johns Creek. He opted for early retirement in 1989, and after several years of traveling the fifty United States and Canada, a time during which he and Kathy took their pre-teen grandson Michael on road trips across the nation and ultimately to view the wonders of Alaska, he then spent thirteen years working as a tax professional for the H&R Block Corporation. During the years at H&R Block, he assembled a loyal following of many clients and became an Enrolled Agent, the sought-after and highest certification of proficiency recognized by the Internal Revenue Service.

In 2005, the author and his youngest natural sibling, Bruce, decided to research and write the history of their father's death house experiences for the Kelly family. Many of the wives, grandkids, and great-grandchildren were largely unaware of that period of the Reverend Kelly's ministry, the man they all loved and called "Pap" or "Grand-pap." During the prolonged period of sporadic research, it was realized the long dormant stories of our chaplain father's execution experiences were intensely reflective of the societal conditions of the 1920s, 1930s, and 1940s. As those stories came back to life, it was decided that they should be published and shared with others.

Included in the narrative, even though Chaplain Kelly was either minimally or not involved, are chapters on the murder of the penitentiary guard official, Captain J. Olin Sanders, and the atheist World War II soldier, John Robinson. Those two cases, especially the Depression era murder of the guard captain and the subsequent execution of his six murderers, are significant to the criminal history of South Carolina. The Bigham case, in which the Reverend Kelly became involved with Ed Bigham's parole, dominated the headlines during the 1920s. The three chapters are included because of the added context they bring to the narrative.

The Captain Sanders murder inundated the news stories during the 1930s, and the infamous Logue case dictated the headlines, even over the World War II headlines and reports, during the early 1940s.

The author is a lay student of American and military history, and the love of those subjects whetted the desire to dig deeply into the criminal history of our nation and of the state of South Carolina during the period immediately preceding the Civil Rights era, the era when the black man's legitimate grievances were finally recognized and corrective action started.

Executed Inmates Interred in Tickleberry While the Reverend Kelly was Chaplain at the Prison:

Name	Date Buried at Tickleberry
*Charlie Smith	November 29, 1946
Lewis Scott	December 20, 1946
Rose Marie Stinette	January 17, 1947
John Dickerson	May 02, 1947
J.C. Sims	July 11, 1947
Willie Pooler	August 01, 1947

* PRISON RECORDS STATE that Charlie Smith's body was claimed by his wife and that he was returned home for burial. Newspaper accounts relate the body was not claimed and that Smith's body was interred in Tickleberry. There is nothing in the Reverend Kelly's notes concerning Smith's burial.

Executions Witnessed by Chaplain C. M. Kelly

Name	Crime	Age	Race	Date
Hugh Evans	Rape	22	White	02/07/1941
Willis Evans	Rape	20	White	02/07/1941
Sue Logue	Murder	43	White	01/15/1943
George Logue	Murder	53	White	01/15/1943
Clarence Bagwell	Murder	34	White	01/15/1943
Jesse Jones	Murder	19	Black	04/02/1943
Johnnie Sims	Murder	18	Black	07/16/1943
Sylvester McKinney	Murder	21	Black	07/16/1943
Sammie Osborne	Murder	18	Black	11/19/1943
Frank Timmons	Assault W/	19	Black	05/12/1944
George Stinney Jr.	Murder	14	Black	06/16/1944
Bruce Hamilton	Assault W/	21	Black	06/16/1944
* Hurley Jones	Rape	22	Black	11/03/1944
** Bessie M. Williams	Murder	19	Black	12/29/1944
** Ralph Thompson	Murder	18	Black	12/29/1944
** Melvin Wade	Rape	24	Black	12/29/1944
Charles Gilstrap	Rape	28	White	02/09/1945
George Carter	Assault/W	29	Black	12/14/1945
Wash Pringle	Rape	32	Black	01/25/1946
Louis Gatlin	Rape	20	Black	07/19/1946
Charlie Smith	Murder	66	Black	11/29/1946
Junius A. Judge	Murder	25	Black	12/20/1946
Lewis Scott	Murder	28	Black	12/20/1946
Cleve Covington	Murder	26	Black	01/03/1947
Rose M. Stinette	Murder	40	Black	01/17/1947
Robert Jordan	Murder	21	Black	02/14/1947
Talmadge Haggins	Murder	25	Black	04/18/1947
Freddie Jones	Murder	19	Black	04/25/1947
John Dickerson	Murder	36	Black	05/02/1947

William A. Davis	Rape	24	Black	06/20/1947
J. C. Sims	Murder	36	Black	07/11/1947
Bert Grant Jr.	Rape	18	Black	07/25/1947
William Pooler	Rape	19	Black	08/01/1947
Leonard A. Pringle	Murder	25	Black	08/15/1947
Ernest Willis	Murder	26	Black	08/15/1947

* CHAPLAIN KELLY WAS absent and did not witness the execution of Hurley Jones. He arranged for the Rev. Dr. C. F. Wimberly to be present.

** THE EXECUTIONS OF Bessie M. Williams, Ralph Thompson and Melvin Wade were in the North Carolina gas chamber.

Sources Used for Research

South Caroliniana Library at the University of South Carolina

South Carolina State Supreme Court Library

South Carolina Department of Archives and History

Letters from the Files of Governors Olin D. Johnston and Ransome J. Williams

Chaplain C. M. Kelly's Notes

Verbal or Written Contributions from members of the Bagwell Family, Mr. Marshall Loftis, the Reverend Billy Patterson, Ms. Geraldine Paxton and a Timmerman relative.

Newspapers: The following newspapers are on file at the South Caroliniana Library at the University of South Carolina, in Columbia. Those files were used extensively during research, and it is with the permission of the South Caroliniana Library that the listed sources were referenced and quoted in many chapters throughout the book.

The Columbia Record

The Charleston News and Courier

The Edgefield Advertiser

The Florence Morning News

The Greenville News

The Spartanburg Herald

The State

The Sumter Daily News

CPSIA information can be obtained at www.ICGtesting.com
Printed in the USA
BVOW08s0620170716

455843BV00001B/66/P